There's
HOPE
for the
HURTING

D1563491

Richard Lee

HARVEST HOUSE PUBLISHERS
Eugene, Oregon 97402

THERE'S HOPE FOR THE HURTING

Copyright © 1994 by Harvest House Publishers
Eugene, Oregon 97402

Library of Congress Cataloging-in-Publication Data

Lee, Richard, 1946–
    There's hope for the hurting / Richard Lee.
        p.   cm.
    ISBN 1-56507-164-6
    1. Christian life.   2. Consolation.   I. Title.
II. Title: There is hope for the hurting.
BV4501.2.L42536   1994
248.8'6—dc20   94-15731
                                                       CIP

*Dedicated to
the friends and supporters
of There's Hope Ministries,
who through their faithfulness week by week
help us carry the message
of hope to the world.*

About the Author

Dr. Richard Lee is the senior pastor of Rehoboth Baptist Church in Atlanta, one of the nation's largest churches, and speaker on the national telecast "There's Hope!" His ministry is biblical, practical, and targeted to the needs of people in all walks of life today. Dr. Lee holds Bachelor of Arts, Master of Divinity, Doctor of Ministry, and Doctor of Law degrees, and is the author of seven books, including *Angels of Deceit* with Ed Hindson.

CONTENTS

Part 1

Hope for Your Troubles

1

Where Is God
When I
Need Him Most?

I have in my hand a letter I received not long ago. Perhaps you can identify with the feelings shared by the person who wrote it:

> Dear Pastor Lee,
>
> I am very discouraged and downhearted at this time. I'm a middle-aged man who is in good health. Because of problems in my field of work, I've been unemployed for many months now. I can get no unemployment compensation. My wife has been sick for a long time, and it is evident she will never work again. I need a job. I want a job that will support us, but it's just not there. Often I think of suicide, but I believe that is wrong. I pray and I try, but nothing seems to happen.
>
> Where is God, Pastor? I've been a Christian for forty years, but I see no light at the end of my tunnel. Pastor, where is God when I need Him the most?

I have to admit that is a good question. It is one we all ask ourselves sooner or later. No matter how exciting your Christian walk may be now or may have been in the past, most of us come to those difficult moments where we do not know for sure which way to turn. When we are sick or lonely or unemployed, these feelings of inadequacy come over us like a dark shadow of despair which seems to reach into every crevice of our being. It asks us the haunting question: Where is God in all this?

Things can seem to go wrong even when we are doing everything we can to live right. You don't have to be living in deliberate sin and shaking your fist in the face of God for something to go wrong. The truth is that bad things do happen to good people. If you haven't yet experienced this for yourself (and in time you will), you surely know someone else who has. Problems are a part of the reality of life. No one is immune to them. They come upon all of us sooner or later.

"But where is God in the middle of my problems?" people often ask. The answer to that is implied in the question itself. He is right where He said He would be—in the middle of our problems. He is never absent from our troubles. He is right there ready to help us handle them. That is why the apostle Paul wrote that He "comforts us in *all* our troubles" (2 Corinthians 1:4 NIV, emphasis added). He does not necessarily always keep us from trouble.

Finding God When You Really Need Him

Lucy in the "Peanuts" comic strip was complaining about her problems. Charlie Brown tried to comfort her by saying, "Lucy, into life a little rain must fall. Besides, life will always have its ups and downs." To this Lucy replied, "But Charlie Brown, I don't want any ups and downs! All I want is ups and ups and ups!" Most of us want just the "ups" of life, but unfortunately we cannot isolate one truth about life, such as God's blessings, from another truth, such as God's justice. Every attribute of God works in perfect harmony with every other attribute. We cannot select one and avoid the other any more than we can choose one Scripture and neglect others.

Some time ago, I was visited by a dear lady who told me that she felt God had abandoned her. "No matter how hard I pray," she said, "God just doesn't answer me."

"What kind of answer are you expecting?" I asked.

"One that says yes to what I feel I need, of course," she replied abruptly.

"Well, my understanding is that God doesn't always say yes," I suggested. "Sometimes He tells us no for our own good."

"But that's not what I want to hear," she stated.

"I know it may not be what you *want* to hear," I answered, "but it just may be what you *need* to hear!"

Nowhere does God promise to always give us all that we want. In fact, the Scripture warns us that if we ask for something with the wrong motive, we can be sure that we won't get it. How many times have you prayed selfishly for something that, if God had given it to you, it would have ruined you? Remember, God is too wise to help us destroy ourselves with selfish desires.

If you really want to find God's answers to your troubles, turn to His Word. The Bible is filled with principles for living, and in it we find the answers to the questions that so often trouble our souls. Seeking God is not some vague, mystical experience. Rather, it is a deliberate search for truth in His revealed Word.

God is always there in our darkest hours. Even when we think all is going wrong, He is still at work in us. We simply need to learn to see His hand at work in our lives. Consider these thoughts when you seem to be wondering where God is in your situation.

When Your Request Is Wrong, God Is Denying You

James 4:3 says, "Ye ask, and receive not, because ye ask amiss." To "ask amiss" means to ask with the wrong motives. When your motive for asking is not right, God will not grant your requests. This doesn't mean He has deserted you. He is still there, but He is denying your request for your own good. You cannot expect God to contradict His own wisdom and give you something that is not good for you simply because you demand it.

God is too wise to be fooled by our clever devices and our petty insistence that we get our own way. He is omniscient, or all-knowing. He knows all about us. Our past, as well as our future, is ever present before the mind of God. How could a loving God who knows everything that ever will be answer yes to our prayers if He knows that answer will ultimately hurt us?

A classic example of this kind of request is found in 1 Kings 19:1-4. Elijah the prophet was God's spokesman. He had called down the fire of God on the altar on Mount Carmel. He had slain the prophets of Baal and called down judgment on the royal family of Israel. But when wicked Queen Jezebel determined to kill him, he fled for his life. He escaped into the wilderness and took shelter under a juniper tree. There, in total exhaustion, he begged God to take his life. But it was a prayer God refused to answer.

Elijah didn't really want to die. If that had been the case, he could just as well have stayed in town; Jezebel would have been glad to accommodate him. Elijah was simply looking for an easy way out of his troubles. He wanted to pull the ejection cord and catapult out the escape hatch of life. But God said no for his own good.

We are all often guilty of the same kind of selfish requests. We want God to bail us out of our troubles— troubles that He wants to use to mold and shape our lives. In reality, He is often protecting us from our own selfishness and greed. When He refuses to answer our prayers that are prompted by wrong motives, He is actually proving that He is there when we need Him most to say no for our own good.

When Your Timing Is Wrong, God Is Delaying You

In Ecclesiastes 3:1, we read, "To every thing there is a season, and a time to every purpose under the heaven." Timing is crucial to almost everything in life. This is especially true in athletics. It does not matter how much physical ability an athlete has—he will not be a winner if he cannot achieve the proper timing. There have been many baseball players, for example, who had the strength to hit home runs yet could not time the swing of their bat to meet the ball properly, and they failed to make it in baseball.

This principle is often true in our daily lives. Even when we desire something that is within the will of God, we must be willing to wait for His timing to bring it to pass. God never promised to answer our prayers on *our* timetable. There is not one guarantee in Scripture that He will always give us what we want when we want it. Don't ever think that you can just snap your fingers and God will jump right then and answer your request. If He did that, you would be God and He would be your servant. It just doesn't work that way.

Unfortunately, many people think that God exists simply to take care of their needs. They treat Him as though He were a puppet attached to some strings. When they pull the strings, they expect Him to get moving. I remember hearing someone say, "I've got the faith, He's got the promises, so He has to answer me." That kind of mentality treats God like a heavenly vending machine. Some people think all they have to do is stick in a prayer, pull the promise knob, and out pops a miracle.

We live in an instantaneous age. We want everything right now. That is why we have fast food and instant coffee. Our generation knows little or nothing about delayed gratification. Not long ago, people had to wait a long time to be able to afford something they wanted. Now we just lay down a credit card and take it home today.

When we turn to God in prayer, we expect the same instant results. Unfortunately, that is not how God works.

He moves on His schedule, not ours. He is our Father and we are His children. We had better not forget how that relationship works. We don't set the agenda. He does. The sooner we realize that all of God's blessings aren't sent by Federal Express, the better we will be able to appreciate and accept His timing.

Trust in the truth
that God will answer your prayers
in time, on time.

And remember, God's timing is always crucial to our ultimate well-being. God is the one who made time. He knows us best and always operates on schedule. When we are in a holding pattern, it does not mean that God is not there, but that He is delaying the answer for our own good. Sometimes we will find ourselves in a divine time delay. Don't give up at those times. Trust in the truth that God will answer in time, on time, when the time is right.

When Your Course Is Wrong, God Is Directing You

When we get off course in life, God lovingly, yet firmly, directs us back on the proper path. For some of us, this happens frequently. For others, this is an occasional experience. But for all of us, it is a necessary process in order to keep us in line with His will. When things are going well, we tend to pay little attention to the priorities of our lives. But when the bottom falls out, God can get our attention in a hurry. In times of trouble we are usually quick to examine ourselves and seek His direction.

Jonah was a prophet of God who got off the right course. God had commanded him to go east to Nineveh, the Assyrian capital, to preach to the enemies of Israel. Instead, Jonah fled in the opposite direction. He went down to the Mediterranean seacoast town of Joppa and took a ship headed west to Tarshish. Exhausted, he fell sound asleep in the ship, only to be awakened by a violent storm. The Bible declares that God sent the storm because Jonah was running away from God's will. In desperation, and perhaps because of self-inflicted guilt, Jonah told the mariners to throw him overboard to appease the wrath of God.

I have met a lot of people in my lifetime who were just like Jonah. They were moving in a direction opposite to God's will for their lives, and He sent along a storm to get their attention. But some, instead of repenting and changing direction, wanted to end it all through a self-destructive act. That, however, is never the right answer to your problems. God is greater than that. He has plans and purposes for you that are far more grand in their design than to simply leave you on the trash heap of life.

At the moment of Jonah's desperation, the Bible says, "The LORD had prepared a great fish" (Jonah 1:17). Jonah wasn't swallowed by accident, but by divine purpose. There, inside that uniquely prepared vehicle of God's grace, Jonah cried out to God in prayer. The Bible says, "*Then* Jonah prayed" (2:1, emphasis added). He had not prayed when he decided to run away. Nor had he prayed when he first entered the ship and fell asleep. But now, *in* the depth of his troubles, he called out to God, and God redirected his course.

Often you and I are a lot like Jonah. We know what God wants us to do, but we are unwilling to do it. In our rebellion, we devise our clever plans to exclude God from our lives and run off in our own direction. When we think we have escaped His notice, God sends the storms to get our attention. Why? Because He knows that trouble will cause us to reexamine our priorities and put our lives back on course with His will and purpose.

When the difficulties of life come your way, don't give up on God. He hasn't forsaken you. Many times He is right there *in* all the troubles trying to get your attention. Turn to Him, seek His face, and follow His direction for your life. As you do, you will experience the assurance of His presence, and the peace of His purpose will finally be accomplished in your life.

When Your Life Is Wrong, God Is Disciplining You

You and I cannot sin and get away with it. God always holds us accountable for our actions. He is our heavenly Father, and like any good father, He disciplines His children. That does not mean He enjoys disciplining us, but He does so because He knows it is ultimately for our good.

My father was a strong disciplinarian. He did it the old-fashioned way by turning me over his knee and spanking me. I clearly remember that when he spanked me, he would always say, "Son, this hurts me more than it does you." At times I wanted to suggest to him that we trade places if it hurt him so much!

But I never could understand or appreciate what he meant by that remark until I became a father myself. Then when my own children would misbehave and I had to discipline them for their wrongdoing, it often broke my heart to have to give them the "rod of correction." I loved my children, and my heart ached for them. Yet, I knew they needed to be disciplined in order to change their direction in life.

When God disciplines us, I believe He does so with a broken heart. He gets no pleasure out of the process, but love compels Him to do it for our sake. And, through the whole process, He knows He is risking our displeasure. When I discipline my children, I am laying my reputation on the line with them. I am risking their anger. They may turn against me, but I am compelled to do what is right for their ultimate good. God operates the same way. He knows that we may rebel against Him in our innermost being, but

He risks disciplining us because He loves us. He is willing to sacrifice our opinion of Him for our own benefit.

When we are under God's discipline, He is there correcting us. He has not forsaken us, nor has He abandoned us. The Bible reminds us, "No chastening for the present seemeth to be joyous, but grievous: nevertheless afterward it yieldeth the peaceable fruit of righteousness" (Hebrews 12:11). No matter what you are going through, God is in control of the process, and afterwards it will be worthwhile.

Through It All, God Is Developing You

We are all in a process of spiritual development. We are progressing in our walk with God. The Bible calls this process sanctification. It means that we are gradually and progressively being conformed to the image of Christ. In Philippians 1:6, the apostle Paul put it this way: "Being confident of this very thing, that he which hath begun a good work in you will perform it until the day of Jesus Christ." If God has started a work in your life, He will complete it and bring it to fruition.

God will never put
any more pressure on us
than we can bear.

Many have the idea that they have to become perfect overnight. But the process of sanctification is a slow one. Do not try to heal yourself before you call the Doctor. Come to Jesus, and He will help you with your problems. So many people try to save themselves before they come to the Savior. They try to clean up before they come. You might as well try to get full before you eat. You might as well say, "I will never get in the water until I know how to swim," or, "I will never touch a piano until I know how to play."

None of us have attained perfection. We are all pilgrims journeying through this world on the road of life. We have not yet arrived at our celestial destination, but we are on our way. Our path may be filled with many obstacles and pitfalls, but through it all, the Savior guides us. No matter what process of God's grace you find operative in your life at this time, He is there and He is at work.

In Romans 5:3, the apostle Paul urges us to "glory in tribulations [troubles] also: knowing that tribulation worketh patience." The word "glory" in the original Greek text means "rejoice." So we are to rejoice in our troubles because we know that God is at work in our lives producing His qualities of patience and endurance.

What the word "patience" describes here is not an attitude of simply waiting for something to happen, but the ability to endure under a tremendous load. And the term "tribulation" comes from the Greek word that means to "squash" or "smash." In New Testament times, the Romans commonly executed their victims by piling heavy stones upon them until they died. What the apostle Paul is telling us is that we can endure under the heavy load of life because God will never put any more pressure on us than we can bear. Therefore, we can rejoice despite our pressures because God is greater than all our problems.

I can recall many times early in my ministry when I would visit elderly saints who had known the Lord for many years. "Isn't God good?" one of them would say, despite a terminal illness or a long period of loneliness. I would think, *How can you have the courage to talk about God's goodness right in the middle of your suffering?* But what I had yet to realize was that they had learned that God's grace was greater than all their troubles. They knew that in spite of all the problems of life, God was with them. This is one of the great lessons of life we all must learn. God is at work even in our greatest difficulties. When we wonder where He is, He is right there, molding us into the image of His Son.

You may feel that God has forsaken you for the moment, but He has not! He has promised never to leave you nor forsake you (*see* Hebrews 13:5). In His temporary silence, He is still speaking to the ears of your soul. Even now, His denials, delays, and redirections are all part of His answers to your prayers.

2

Don't
Dodge the Fire

*T*rouble is something everybody has and nobody seems to want. But the trouble with trouble is not the trouble itself but the way we handle it. One young man loses his girlfriend and jumps off a bridge, committing suicide. Another young man loses his girlfriend, writes a song about it, and makes a million dollars! The difference is in the way you treat the problems of life.

In the third chapter of Daniel, we read the story of three Hebrew boys: Shadrach, Meshach, and Abednego. They had been taken captive to Babylon as teenagers along with another young man by the name of Daniel. While in Babylon, the four of them were placed in a training school for three years to prepare them for government service under the king of Babylon. It was during this time that they had refused to eat the meat or drink the wine which the king had provided for them because they felt it was in violation of their beliefs and convictions. Having taken a stand for righteousness, they had already come under criticism from some of the Babylonian officials. However, God blessed them, and they were the most outstanding students in their graduating class. By the time we get to the end of Daniel 2,

Daniel himself has risen to the position of prime minister to the king.

In Daniel 3:1 we read that Nebuchadnezzar the king of Babylon ordered a golden statue to be erected. He wanted all of his people to bow down and worship this image. Nowhere in this account do we read Daniel's name; apparently he had been sent away on business. Perhaps the king knew Daniel would never bow to the statue, so out of his high regard for Daniel, he may have sent him away.

Then came the day for the celebration and worship of the idol. The king's plan was simple: When the musicians played, all the nation would bow before the golden idol. All went well as the music loudly sounded. Suddenly, all of the nation went to its knees—that is, except three young Jews. You can guess who they were: Shadrach, Meshach, and Abednego!

Nebuchadnezzar was infuriated by their refusal to worship the idol, but he gave them another chance to bow before the image. When they politely refused to do so, he commanded that they be thrown into a fiery furnace which had been heated seven times hotter than ever before.

Talk about trouble—it can't get much worse than this! Surely it's true that all of us get into a mess sooner or later in our lives. But few of us will ever have to face the kind of trouble these young men faced on that day. They had taken a stand for their beliefs and convictions, and now they were being called upon to pay for it. It is one thing to claim to believe something, and it is an entirely different matter to be willing to die for it. These three young men had taken such a stand. They had faced the king of the greatest nation in the world and told him that they would not bow to his demands regardless of the consequences. Yet in the midst of their troubles, God delivered them.

God Will Get You Through

You don't have to be in the kind of trouble these three young Hebrew teenagers found themselves in to appreciate the power of God's deliverance. But whatever your difficulties are, it is good to know that there is always deliverance available from God. If you are struggling right now with some great problem in your life, let me remind you that it is not likely that it is as severe as what these three men faced. And the same God who delivered them can deliver you as well.

Shadrach, Meshach, and Abednego were convinced that God was in control of their lives. At their moment of greatest need they were willing to trust themselves to His sovereign will. That is why they were able to face Nebuchadnezzar and say:

> Our God whom we serve is able to deliver
> us from the burning fiery furnace, and he will
> deliver us out of thine hand, O king. But if not,
> be it known unto thee, O king, that we will not
> serve thy gods, nor worship the golden image
> which thou hast set up (Daniel 3:17-18).

On the one hand, they were expressing their faith and confidence in God's power to deliver them. But on the other hand, they were not presuming upon His will to deliver them. In other words, their attitude was one of perfect balance and submission to the will of God. They were saying that they believed that God had the power to deliver them if He chose to do so, but even if He did not so choose, they would still serve Him. That is the kind of attitude which reveals an individual's confidence in the power and purposes of God. It is a kind of confidence which most people know little about today. We tend to want to manipulate the will of God and to convince Him that He should do it our way.

If you were to ask the average person on the street, "Who do you think is running the world?" most of them would give some kind of political response. They would refer to the president of the United States or the Soviet

Union or some other political figure. The tragedy is that many politicians do not think that God is in control. They seldom use the name of God except in vain. In the business world, the average person does not believe that God is in control. Rarely do businesses begin the day with a word of prayer and request God's blessing and guidance upon their efforts. While there are always exceptions, the tragedy is that most people in the influential positions in our nation are not at all convinced that God can help them. One of our national leaders recently said that as a nation, we control our own destiny. I am not sure that this line of reasoning is fully true. While we certainly have a responsibility for our national affairs, we cannot overlook the fact that God still rules in those affairs.

God Controls Your Life

Interestingly, the book of Daniel opens with the Babylonian invasion of Judah. In that invasion the Babylonians took a number of the children of Israel into captivity, including Daniel and his three friends. But in that opening chapter, the prophet makes the statement, "The Lord gave

*God knows what is going to happen
before it happens.*

Jehoiakim, king of Judah into his [Nebuchadnezzar's] hand" (Daniel 1:2). The Scripture makes it clear that Nebuchadnezzar was successful only as far as God allowed him to succeed. While his army may have been militarily superior, it was not the only key to his victory. Daniel and his friends understood that they were not in Babylon by chance. God had put them there. He was in control of the situation from the beginning.

The Bible tells us that God knows what is going to happen before it happens. It is that knowledge that is the basis of all predictive prophecy in Scripture. God can tell the future because He controls the future. He knew from the beginning that the people of Judah would be conquered by the Babylonians. He knew that they would be taken into captivity. On many occasions He had predicted the deportation in advance. He had also predicted the eventual deliverance of His people and their return to the Promised Land. Shadrach, Meshach, and Abednego knew those promises. They understood that their captivity was for a specific purpose—that it fulfilled the will of God. So even in their moments of desperation, they did not turn against the God whom they knew to be in control of the whole world.

At the Point of Your Need

God knew what kind of persecution His children were facing and what He would have to do to deliver them out of it. At this point we read,

> And these three men, Shadrach, Meshach, and Abednego, fell down bound into the midst of the burning fiery furnace. Then Nebuchadnezzar the king was astoni[sh]ed, and rose up in haste, and spake, and said unto his counsellors, Did not we cast three men bound into the midst of the fire? They answered and said unto the king, True, O king. He answered and said, Lo, I see four men loose, walking in the midst of the fire, and they have no hurt; and the form of the fourth is like the Son of God (Daniel 3:23-25).

The fiery furnace, the intensity of the heat, and the anger of Nebuchadnezzar were all human efforts to thwart the will of God. But He overcame them all! At the moment of His children's greatest need, He sent His Son to deliver them from the fire. In so doing, God gives us a beautiful picture of His working in our lives. He does not always choose to keep us from the fire, but often brings about our deliverance while we are in the fire itself.

If God could deliver these young men from a fiery furnace, it should seem evident He can deliver us from whatever trouble we find ourselves in. He is still in control of this world. Satan may do all he can to disrupt the process, but God is still in control. He can even use the wrath of men to bring praise to Himself. That is exactly what God did in this situation. Nebuchadnezzar had responded in anger and had made a decision that was completely irrational. He knew these young men were of the highest possible intellect and ability, yet he chose to try to destroy them anyway. But his angry decision was reversed by the power of God.

The sooner we understand that God is the one who has final authority over all, the better off we will be. We can avoid wasting a lot of energy worrying about things that are already under His control. As believers, we know that God is working all things together for our good (Romans 8:28). While God is not the source of our troubles, He can use those troubles and overrule them to produce good results in our lives. That means no matter what difficulties life throws at us, God can use them for good. I am convinced that even when we stray from His will and make serious mistakes, God can overrule our failures and problems to bring about His will in our lives. He may use those difficulties to teach us great lessons and to bring us to a point of repentance, but ultimately, He can also use them to produce a wonderful result that only He could bring to pass. It is only when we understand the sovereign control of God that we can really trust Him with the everyday details of our lives.

Someone may say, "What if I get into trouble and God doesn't come through?" Such thinking is faulty; who said that God has to come through the way *we* want Him to? If I have the confidence that God truly knows what is best for my life and that He has the power to overrule anything for my own good, then I must believe that He has already properly prepared to come through on my behalf. If, on the other hand, I assume that God must meet my needs in a way that I have predetermined, then I am going to be disappointed.

We cannot judge God on a performance basis. If something succeeds from the perspective of our fleshly, materialistic eyes, we tend to say that God was in it. The truth is that He may not have been in it at all. The success may simply be a work of human effort and nothing more. On the other hand, when God appears to be inactive, the truth is that He may well be accomplishing a greater purpose than we could ever have imagined. The mature believer understands that and is willing to say, "I trust You, Lord, no matter what the circumstances may be."

If there was ever a person who had a right to give up on God, it was certainly Job. He lost everything he had, including his children and health. In his most desperate moment, his wife abandoned him and his three friends condemned him. Yet Job remained confident in the sovereign purposes of God. In the face of great personal tragedy he said, "Though he slay me, yet will I trust in him" (Job 13:15). Despite his circumstances, Job's faith remained firm in God.

In the Furnace of Affliction

As God works in our lives, He often reveals His will and purposes to us in the very circumstances in which we are struggling. He wants us to understand that He has not given up on us. He also makes it clear that His sovereign power is still at work in our lives no matter what those circumstances may be.

Consider once again King Nebuchadnezzar. Imagine the great confrontation which was about to take place between this human king and the sovereign God. Nebuchad-nezzar was the leader of the greatest nation on the face of the earth at that time. He was an absolute autocrat whose very word was law. In his pride, he had decided to build a huge image overlaid with pure gold. The 90-foot structure was built on the great plain outside the city where it could be seen for many miles. When the image was completed, Nebuchadnezzar assembled all the pomp that Babylon could provide to make a great display of his authority. A band was on hand to play and all of the officials and dignitaries of the empire were there—except Daniel. Perhaps Nebuchadnezzar thought that the other three would not take a stand without him. But he could not have been more wrong. The same spiritual qualities which Daniel possessed were also a reality in the lives of these three young men. When they took their stand against the king, they were taking their stand for God. I am convinced that when we are willing to do that, God will not overlook our needs.

These young adults were men of conviction and maturity. They did not demand that God deliver them. They did not make any ridiculous promises based on their own merit or even on their own faith. They were fully prepared to die for what they believed in, even though they understood that God had the power to deliver them if He chose to do so. And if He chose otherwise, they wanted Nebuchadnezzar to know that they would not succumb to the pressure which he had placed on them. I do not know what they thought as they listened to the decree of judgment pronounced against them; I am not certain how they might have felt as the soldiers carried them up the outside steps to the top of that domed furnace. But every indication of the text would seem to tell us that they faced their punishment with absolute confidence in the power of God.

The Bible tells us that Nebuchadnezzar's soldiers tied the men up in their own stockings and threw them into the fire through the opening at the top of the furnace. The fire was so intense that the heat and smoke overcame the soldiers and burned them alive as they tried to flee. In the meantime, the three Hebrews landed in the middle of the fire, where they should have been destroyed instantly. Instead, not a hair on their heads was even singed. God had come to reveal His faithfulness to them.

The Bible tells us that Nebuchadnezzar was totally astonished when he realized that the fire had not destroyed the three young men. He apparently ran to a side entrance to the furnace where he could see that the men were walking around unhurt in the midst of the fire. What's more, he saw a fourth person with them in the furnace.

While God did not choose to deliver them *from* the fire, He did choose to deliver them *in* the fire. He wanted to show His power to all of the people who were assembled at the great event. Therefore, He allowed the three men to be thrown into the furnace.

*Problems have a way
of bringing us closer to God.*

There are so many times in our lives that we want to tell God how to solve our problems. We want to make sure that He is not going to allow us to be thrown into the furnace, so to speak. We claim that we believe in His deliverance, but we want Him to deliver us before we face any trouble. In contrast, the Scriptures clearly tell us that, more often than not, God will deliver us *in* our troubles rather than *from* our troubles. This concept is clearly stated in 2 Corinthians 1:4, where the apostle Paul says that God "comforteth us in all our tribulation, that we may be able to comfort them which are in any trouble." God allowed these young men to stay in the furnace just long enough for them to realize the greatness of His deliverance. He also allowed them to stay in long enough for the Babylonians to realize it as well.

I know that it is never fun to go through the furnace of persecution and suffering, but when you do, you can be assured that God is with you. Problems help to knock away our pride, they cause us to lose our self-dependence, and more than anything else, they tend to bring us closer to God. When everything is going well for us we tend not to draw near to God nearly so much as when everything is going wrong.

As a pastor I have watched many people over the years who have developed a self-sufficient attitude when life was going their way. But when the bottom fell out or they found themselves flat on their back, it was a totally different story. That's when they began to cry out to God to meet their needs. Suddenly those who had little time for God found themselves spending much time with Him.

Now, I am not suggesting that God is heartless in the manner in which He deals with us. I do not believe that He wants to inflict suffering on us in order to get us to love or trust Him. Rather, I am convinced that the sufferings and difficulties of life are a part of life itself. They are going to come our way whether God uses them or not. The difference for the Christian is that he understands that God uses those experiences for good and not for evil. The believer knows that no matter what has gone wrong on the surface of circumstances, God is still at work in the depth of his life.

Not only did the Hebrew children receive their revelation of deliverance in the furnace, but they also received a revelation of the Deliverer. It has been debated by commentators whether the fourth figure was an angel or if it was Christ Himself. I personally believe that it must have been Christ. Notice that when Nebuchadnezzar called to them to come out of the furnace, they did not respond immediately. Most of us would have been glad to go running out of the furnace, but these men seemed content to stay in there because of who was with them. The king had to beg them to come out. I believe that they were excited not so much about being in the furnace as they were excited about who was in the furnace with them.

I would rather be in a fiery furnace with Christ than in a place of luxury without Him. I would rather be in trouble with Jesus than appear to have my life together and not have Him in my life at all. While He is always present in the lives of His children, we often find ourselves closest to Him in our times of trouble. It is then that we plead with Him not to leave or forsake us. It is then that we call upon Him with a heart of fervency. It is then that we desperately reach out to Him for help and guidance and direction. And the wonderful truth of Scripture is that it is also then that He stands by us and delivers us to His glory and honor.

Overcoming the Flames

The results of the suffering of these three Hebrews were incredible. First, these men made an indelible impression upon Nebuchadnezzar himself. This impression may well have led to the king's subsequent conversion, which is recorded in Daniel 3:28-29. When Shadrach, Meshach, and Abednego came out of the fiery furnace, the Bible says, they were not burned, nor was there even the smell of fire or smoke upon them. Nebuchadnezzar was so stunned that he immediately blessed the God of Shadrach, Meshach, and Abednego and gave testimony to His power to deliver. Second, the king made a decree that no one could speak anything amiss against God because of His power to deliver. And third, he promoted Shadrach, Meshach, and Abednego to greater authority and responsibility in the province of Babylon.

Greater results could not have come from a more catastrophic beginning. For a few moments, it must have seemed that the heavens were silent and that God had not chosen to deliver His children. But when He did deliver them, He did it with such great power that everyone was convinced that He was indeed God. This is the key that we must learn to understand in our own lives. We cannot put God on our timetable, nor can we insist that He meet our every demand. While we can claim His promises and trust Him to sustain us, at the same time we must understand that He knows better what we really need in our lives. God's perspective is one that is eternal. He sees your life from beginning to end and He knows what will best benefit you in the long run.

The God who loved you enough to save you loves you enough to continue working in you.

When you get to a place in your life where you are in the middle of trouble and you feel that you are all alone, remember that God is still there. He is ever present in our lives and He is constantly at work on our behalf. The Bible promises us, "Being confident of this very thing, that he which hath begun a good work in you will perform it until the day of Jesus Christ" (Philippians 1:6). When God saved you and brought you into a personal relationship with Himself, He began a work in your life. But that work did not end at salvation. Therefore, you can rest assured that the God who loved you enough to save you loves you enough to continue His work in your life. No matter what problems you may face, God is still in control and He is still at work. With that in mind, you can, if you will, turn life's troublesome fires into triumphant faith.

3

The Truth about Trouble

*A*s I watched the evening news one night, there came the story of a little girl who lived in Toledo, Ohio. She was like most little girls in every way except one. Her parents noticed it when she was just a baby. It seemed that when she hurt herself, she never cried. At first they thought that she was just an unusually brave little girl, but after a while, they began to suspect that something was wrong.

Finally, her mother took her to the doctor. After several days of examination it was discovered that the little girl had a rare disease of the nervous system which caused her not to be able to feel pain. The doctors cautioned her parents that she could never be left alone, for she could injure herself severely and never feel the pain. So you see, even pain can be a gift from God for our protection and good, while the lack of it can be tragic indeed.

But allow me to talk with you about another kind of pain, a pain that we all endure—the pain of trouble. Everyone has troubles. Life is never so simple that one can travel its road without facing pitfalls and obstacles. Life is a journey, not a hundred-yard dash! The journey is often long and difficult, sometimes tedious, and sometimes treacherous. But in spite of its ups and downs, the journey of life is the most exciting adventure of all.

When life brings us the pain of trouble, we need to ask ourselves: Is it possible that this kind of pain can also be for our protection and good? We must identify our troubles, learn to benefit from them, and in turn bring about their solution.

Some troubles are easy to identify. If your car won't start in the morning, or your refrigerator stops running, you automatically know that you have trouble. But other troubles are not that easy to identify. Frequently people know that there is something wrong in their lives, but they simply don't know what it is. Have you ever been angry and couldn't figure out why? Have you ever been filled with worry and unable to pinpoint what it was you were worried about? If so, you know what I'm referring to. Those feelings indicate unidentified trouble.

Whatever your troubles may be,
they are not beyond the reach
of God's love and grace.

There is another kind of trouble that is more common to us. It is the kind that comes along and slaps us in the face, unexpectedly, unannounced, unprepared for, and unwelcomed. Nevertheless, it's there!

If you are struggling with either unidentified or unexpected trouble in your life, let me encourage you by reminding you that you are not alone in your trial. The Bible tells us that Christ has promised He will never leave nor forsake us (Hebrews 13:5). You can depend on His promise. And do not forget that no matter how insurmountable your difficulties may seem, God is greater than all of them put together. I am convinced that God has a specific solution for every problem we face in life. He created us, understands us, and knows best how to meet our deepest needs. Whatever your troubles may be, they are not beyond the reach of God's love and the grasp of His grace.

How We Benefit from Trouble

It has often been said that trouble will either make us better or bitter. The decision is really up to us. One of the most familiar promises in the Bible is Romans 8:28: "We know that all things work together for good to them that love God, to them who are the called according to his purpose." Not only does God work in our lives through the blessings of His grace and goodness to us, but He is also actively at work through our problems and difficulties as well. That is the key to understanding how to overcome your problems. Once you realize that God is at work in your life despite your outward circumstances or even your inner turmoil, you can have the hope of a better life.

One of the great truths about overcoming trouble is that how we respond to trouble is far more important than the trouble itself. It is our response that reveals our innermost character. Anyone can talk a positive line when life is going well. But it's when the problems come and the bottom seems to fall out from beneath us that our true inner self emerges.

Over the years of my ministry, I have observed many individuals and families who were cruising along the road of life, seemingly without a care in the world. They were healthy, happy, and prosperous in every way. They had good jobs, secure marriages, and beautiful children. Everything seemed to point to the ideal situation in their lives. But when the storms of life came (and storms will come), the reality of their life and its values was put on the line. When life comes along and grabs you by the heels, turns you upside down, and gives you a good shaking with an authentic problem, you begin to understand what troubles are really all about.

Unfortunately, some Americans don't even understand what real problems are. They think that because they can't buy a new car, a fur coat, or take a trip to the Bahamas that they have troubles. Whereas someone who has struggled with the deep problems of life will understand that such people aren't facing any real difficulties at all!

Herbert Casson once wrote, "The average man takes life as a trouble. He is in a chronic state of irritation at the whole performance. He does not learn to differentiate between troubles and difficulties, usually, until some real trouble bowls him over. He fusses about pinpricks until a mule kicks him. Then he learns the difference."*

The Bible is filled with examples of people whose lives seemed to be all together. Outwardly, everything was going well and, all of a sudden, the bottom fell out. I think of Job, whom the Bible described as the wealthiest man of the ancient East. He had countless herds and possessions and a wonderful family. But in one day, he lost them all. On top of that, he lost his health and was brought to the point of utter human despair. Here was a man who had done nothing to bring these problems upon himself. He was suffering despite being a good husband, father, and businessman.

I think also of Joseph, who was the apple of his father's eye. If there was ever anyone who seemed to have the right to give up on God and life itself, it was Joseph. Here was a teenager who had done nothing wrong, and yet had been sold into slavery and thrown into jail. But even in jail, Joseph became a model prisoner and rose to a position of leadership and influence. In time, he was able to stand before the pharaoh of Egypt himself and was promoted to the position of top administrative assistant to the king. He is

*Quote taken from *The Supreme Philosophy of Man* by Alfred Armand Montapert. Used by permission.

a beautiful picture of how someone overcame all of the problems and obstacles in his life and rose to the highest position of influence possible at that time.

Later, when Joseph was reunited with his brothers, they expressed concern about his intentions toward them. He explained to them that though they meant their action for evil, "God meant it for good" (Genesis 50:20 NASB). Joseph's understanding of that truth was what enabled him to endure all the injustice that had come into his life. Instead of being crushed by his troubles, he responded to them in a manner that made it clear that his faith and confidence in God was unshaken. He was not overcome with evil, but rather, he overcame evil with good.

Power to Overcome

Only when you and I learn how to face our problems in the way that Joseph did will we ever be able to overcome them positively and effectively. The troubles of life are real; they exist in all of our lives. But in no way does their presence mean that God has forsaken us. Rather, God is at work in our lives no matter what our circumstances may be.

*Let your problems push you to God,
not away from Him.*

We should also *allow our problems to force us to God.* When children fall down and hurt themselves, they automatically turn to their parents for help. Perhaps you can remember doing that as a youngster. You were hurt and needed help, so you ran to a person who you knew loved you and cherished you. I can still remember my mother

Bob Burton

taking me into her arms and saying something to comfort me and soothe my hurts. That is the same way in which we should go to God with all of our problems and trials. He is the one who loves us and cares for us more than anyone else ever could.

Unfortunately, many people let their problems push them away from God. They become bitter and begin to question His love or even His existence. Bitterness will drive us from God. It will cause us to question His love for us and His commitment to us. It will also cause us to focus our attention on the experiences of others instead of causing us to draw closer to God.

If we are really going to face our troubles and learn to benefit from them, we must allow them to draw us closer to God. Even the personal hurts and wrongs that others meant for harm must be handled in such a manner that they turn out for our own good. Often the very things meant to destroy us will push us to the throne of God's grace.

Another truth is that *present troubles teach us to avoid future ones*. One of the proverbs in Scripture asks the question, "Can a man take fire in his bosom, and his clothes not be burned?" (Proverbs 6:27). Unfortunately, there are certain lessons in life that we learn only after we get burned. While truth can be learned by precept, many of us usually learn it by experience. Once you have experienced the terrible consequences of sin, you will learn to avoid it in the future.

Life is a learning process. Along the journey of life God is continually teaching us through our experiences. One of the most foolish things we can do in that journey is to experience the consequences of our mistakes and not learn from them. Sin can be confessed and forgiven, but its effect still lingers in the memory, and hopefully it is the memory of the consequences of that sin that will cause us not to repeat it in the future.

Finally, our troublesome experiences *help us to give wise counsel to others*. No one can counsel you better than someone who has been through the same kind of diffi-culties. No one can help you get out of the valley better than someone who has walked through that same valley. I have found in my own counseling that I can help people better in relation to the problems that I have struggled with myself. Nothing bothers me more than to hear of people who are experts on everyone else's troubles but have never had any of their own. Either they are not being honest about their problems, or they lack the wisdom to help people face the real issues of life but won't admit it.

Strength for the Journey

If we can learn to respond properly to our problems and allow them to draw us closer to God, then they can be turned into spiritual opportunities for growth and min-istry. As we learn to handle the problems of life, we begin to grow spiritually, and as we do so, we become better equipped to help others do the same. In so doing, we turn our difficulties into opportunities for serving the Lord. It is in this sense that you can really learn to benefit from trouble.

If God is greater than our troubles and He can give us the wisdom to face them, then it only stands to reason that we should seek Him for the solutions to our problems. As I have had to face the difficulties of life myself, I have found a simple process of seeking God to be very beneficial to me personally. Let me share it with you.

Meditate on God's Word

The psalmist says, "Thy word is a lamp unto my feet, and a light unto my path" (Psalm 119:105). As we search the Scripture, we soon realize that it is God's manual for life. It is the key to successful living and the source of our under-standing of God's wisdom. This book is filled with the answers to the problems of life. It can teach us how to know God personally, how to love Him intimately, and how to live a victorious and successful life.

Meditation is the act of self-discipline that enables us to concentrate our attention on the Word of God. It is one thing to read the Bible, but it is an entirely different matter to meditate or think deeply upon its truths. It involves more than just a casual reading of the Bible or the mere listening to a sermon. It involves the mental discipline of total concentration upon the truths and principles of Scripture.

The Word of God has often been pictured as seed which must bear fruit in the heart of the believer. As we read the Word of God, the principles of God are planted in our hearts just as seeds are planted in the ground. In time, those principles begin to come to fruition in our lives. As we meditate on those truths, they begin to grow in our hearts. That is the amazing power of the living Word of God, which is illuminated to our minds by the Holy Spirit.

You can plant a seed in the ground, but if it doesn't receive adequate nourishment, it will die. In like manner, many people take the Word of God and read it casually, never meditating upon its truths. In time, they forget what they have read and the seed of the Word fails to come to fruition in their lives.

If you really want to overcome the troubles of life, read the Word of God and quietly meditate upon its principles. As you allow the Spirit of God to illuminate your heart with the truth of God, you will discover that you are growing spiritually despite your outward difficulties. Once you begin this process, do not give it up. Keep disciplining yourself to seek God, and you will find all that He has for you.

Seek God in Prayer

Prayer is communication between man and God. It is not the mere reciting of certain words or phrases which others have deemed appropriate for addressing deity. Real prayer is the heartfelt expression of one's inner being lifted up to the heart of the infinite and personal God Himself. As you read the Word of God, you may want to express its promises and principles back to God in prayer.

Learning to pray was one of the great concerns of Jesus' disciples. They went out of their way to ask Him to teach them how to pray. Their request seems to imply that effective prayer isn't always easy for everyone. As you struggle to find the meaning and purpose of the problems in your life, learn to pour your heart out to God in prayer. Talk to Him just as you would talk to any person you know. Do not worry about saying appropriate words and phrases: Simply pour your heart out to the Lord. Remember, Jesus Himself said that it was the brokenhearted prayer of the publican which God heard, not the prayer of self-righteousness which was expressed by the Pharisee.

Obey the Principles of Scripture

Once you discover truth, you must determine to obey that truth in your life. The Bible speaks clearly to the specific issues of life and tells us what to do to resolve our problems and difficulties. But knowing what the Bible says and doing what it says are two entirely different things. There are some people who *know* scripturally what is right and wrong for their lives, but they will not commit themselves to *do* what is right. Therefore, they can have no hope of solving their problems.

The Bible expresses truth in many different forms. It contains doctrinal statements, narrative stories, poetic expressions, and prophetic pronouncements. But in all of these literary forms, God Himself is speaking to us through the power of His Word. Because of this, we can know Him, know His will for our lives, and yet still fail to obey the truth expressed in His Word. If you really want to overcome your problems, you must be willing to obey the truth of Scripture.

Endure to the End

Endurance is one of the great qualities of life. Just as an athlete endures the physical hardships of a sports contest in order to win the victory, so also must we be willing to do the same in our individual lives.

In a sense, life is a marathon. It contains many twists and turns and can be won only by endurance and dependability. As you run the race of life, no matter what difficulties and obstacles you may face, remember that he who endures to the end is the real winner. In His letters to the seven churches of Asia (Revelation 2–3), our Lord Jesus emphasized the importance of enduring to the end. He has also promised never to leave or forsake us; therefore, we should have every confidence that we can finish the race of life well. As the apostle Paul came to the end of his ministry, despite all of the difficulties he faced, he said, "I have fought a good fight, I have finished my course, I have kept the faith" (2 Timothy 4:7).

He who endures to the end
is the real winner.

You will never make it in life if you become a quitter. No matter what goes wrong—don't give up! When trouble comes your way the value of courage, persistence, and perseverance is demonstrated. It's with that in mind that I want to share with you the endurance of a man we all know. The story of his life might somewhat surprise you; here is his record:

> At age 22—he failed in his business
> At age 23—he was defeated for the legislature
> At age 24—he failed in his business again
> At age 25—he was elected to the legislature

At age 26—his sweetheart died, leaving him heartbroken
At age 27—he suffered a nervous breakdown
At age 29—he was defeated for speaker of the house
At age 31—he was defeated for elector
At age 34—he was defeated for Congress
At age 37—he was elected to Congress
At age 39—he was defeated for Congress
At age 46—he was defeated for the Senate
At age 47—he was defeated for vice president
At age 49—he was defeated for the Senate
At age 51—he was elected president of the United States

Who was this man who refused to quit? This is the record of Abraham Lincoln. His willingness to endure his troubles won him the presidency of the United States.

Unjustly cast into prison, John Bunyan wrote *Pilgrim's Progress* from behind prison bars.

In his old age, Sir Walter Scott penned some of his most famous classics to pay off a half-million-dollar debt for which he was not legally responsible.

Beethoven composed his most soul-stirring symphonies when he was almost totally deaf and his heart was burdened with deep sorrow. Handel and Mozart gave us their most memorable works as they were approaching death.

Martin Luther, hiding in the castle of Wartburg from the enemies who sought to take his life, translated the Bible into language that the humblest peasant could understand.

Blind Fanny Crosby left us hymns full of comfort and inspiration. Helen Keller, out of her blindness, said, "As I walk about my chamber with unsteady feet, my unconquerable soul soars skyward on the wings of an eagle."

What did all these people have in common? They endured. They refused to quit. Whatever your troubles may be, determine in your heart that you will endure and rest assured that God will see you through.

Leave the Rest to God

The Bible says, "Trust in the LORD with all thine heart; and lean not unto thine own understanding. In all thy ways acknowledge him, and he shall direct thy paths" (Proverbs 3:5-6). This passage reminds us that we cannot trust our own wisdom in solving the troubles of life. Rather, there must come a point at which we totally entrust ourselves to the wisdom and sovereignty of God. A sovereign is someone who has the power to do as he wills. While this concept may seem frightful to some, it ought to be a tremendous encouragement to all of us who know the Lord because He is our sovereign *King*. He is all-powerful, all-knowing, all-loving, and all-wise. He will never do anything to harm us, and He will always do everything He can to help us. That is why we need to turn to Him to meet our deepest need.

The real answers to the troubles of life are not found in the advice columns of the newspapers or in the talk shows on TV and the radio. The real answers are found in the Word of God. They are composed of the principles of truth which are expressed in Scripture. As we learn these truths, meditate upon them, and obey them in our daily living, we can learn to face any trouble, knowing that God is on our side.

There is no problem that God cannot solve. He loves you more than you could ever love yourself, and He understands you better than you could ever understand yourself. He knows what you need, when you need it, and why you need it. When those truths sink into our hearts, we are brought to the calm assurance that we can trust God completely. His promises will never fail.

Part 2

*Grace
for Your Trials*

4

When Saints
Get Sick

*A*lmost no one likes to be sick. Americans proved that last year as they consumed over 20,000 tons of aspirin in their efforts to feel better. No matter how successful you may be in other areas, when you are sick it is difficult to enjoy life at all. Therefore, the desire for physical healing is one of the strongest desires human beings can have. When we are not well, we crave wellness. When we are healthy, we hope to continue in good health. But when sickness comes, it is not without significance in the life of the believer.

Sickness is a topic that was dealt with constantly in the New Testament. There were many occasions on which Jesus healed the sick during His earthly ministry. There were times when the early apostles healed people of physical illness. But just as plainly, Scripture also tells us there were times when even great saints of God *did not* receive physical healing.

One of those times is recorded in 2 Corinthians 12:7-10. In this passage the apostle Paul pours out his heart to the Corinthian believers. He acknowledges that he has been suffering from a "thorn in the flesh," which he does not define specifically. He then explains that he asked the Lord three times to remove this illness from him. God's response, however, was to let the illness remain so that His purposes might be fulfilled. Notice how Paul describes his personal trauma over this illness and how he accepts the grace of God as sufficient to sustain him in his weakness:

> And lest I should be exalted above measure through the abundance of the revelations, there was given to me a thorn in the flesh, the messenger of Satan to buffet me, lest I should be exalted above measure. For this thing I besought the Lord thrice, that it might depart from me. And he said unto me, My grace is sufficient for thee: for my strength is made perfect in weakness. Most gladly therefore will I rather glory in my infirmities, that the power of Christ may rest upon me. Therefore I take pleasure in infirmities, in reproaches, in necessities, in persecutions, in distresses for Christ's sake: for when I am weak, then am I strong.

The depth of truth expressed by Paul in this one passage, when truly understood, is more than adequate to help us face the problem of physical illness. There is little doubt that the "thorn in the flesh" to which Paul refers here was a physical illness. He also notes that it was being used by Satan to "buffet" him, meaning that Satan was attempting to use that sickness to discourage him and literally beat down his spirit. Yet through it all, God used this illness to produce genuine humility and an unbelievable level of spiritual maturity in his life. God's answer to Paul was to point him to His sufficient grace, which could enable him not only to endure the suffering but also to use it for God's glory.

What was Paul's reaction to all of this? Instead of becoming bitter because God would not heal him, he was at peace because of his recognition that God was using his illness for His own greater purposes. Paul's response was that he would most gladly glory in his infirmities. Thus, he could say that he received all of the difficulties of his life with gladness, whether they involved physical infirmities or were the result of reproach and persecution. He understood that in his personal weaknesses, the power of God was manifested to make him strong.

Suffering is not a meaningless experience; rather, it has a divine purpose.

In Paul we find the perfect and balanced response to the problem of physical suffering. The apostle makes it clear that he has personally suffered because of these infirmities of the flesh. He does not take the attitude that these things do not bother him at all. Rather, he makes it clear that he was deeply distressed by his physical weaknesses. But, at the same time, he realized that God was at work in his life in spite of these circumstances, and that God would bring about a greater work as a result of them. Therefore, Paul was able to accept that physical suffering has a purpose in the lives of believers. Suffering is not a meaningless experience; rather, it has a divine purpose. Once we understand that, we are able to accept the process by which God has chosen to work in us.

Dealing with Sickness

In Christian circles today there are three basic approaches to dealing with sickness. Each of these contains elements of truth; but when isolated from one another, they lack a balanced approach to the total problem of physical illness. While none of us desire sickness, it is something that most of us will experience. And when it comes, we need to understand why we are suffering, what we are suffering, and the significance it has in our lives.

The Sin Approach

There is one group of believers who are convinced that people are suffering physically because of sin in their lives. They are quick to point out that sickness is a consequence of the fall of man into sin. In other words, with our sin nature comes the inevitable results of that nature—sickness and death. Therefore, they conclude that whenever someone is suffering physically, that person must be under the judgment of God because of sin in his or her life. This was the approach taken by Job's three friends, who supposedly came to comfort him in all of his distress and anxiety. Job had lost his children, his possessions, and his health. When his friends arrived, they began to rebuke him for hiding some unknown sin. Because he was suffering physically, they assumed that he must have committed some terrible deed of which he was unwilling to repent. Job protested that he was innocent, but they did not believe him and continued their criticism. In many ways they were not unlike a lot of misinformed Christians today. When someone has suffered from an illness or an accident, they automatically assume that he or she must have done something wrong to deserve it. That is a terribly judgmental way to live.

The Faith Approach

Next is a group of Christians who believe that no matter what sickness you are experiencing, God wants to heal you—if you will only have enough faith to let Him do it. They are convinced that all sickness is a violation of the will of God. They generally base this conclusion on the belief that sickness is a result of sin and, therefore, God wants to remove it from our lives. They emphasize the importance of exercising faith in the power and promises of God. If you come away from one of their services without being healed, you will likely be told that it is because you did not have enough faith. Thus, they leave you in a state of frustration and disappointment at being unable to generate sufficient faith. The major problem with the "just muster up enough faith" approach is that it simply doesn't work!

The Sovereignty Approach

There is yet a final group of Christians who are convinced that God is sovereign over the experiences of our lives and that if He has chosen to allow us to suffer from sickness, there really isn't anything that we can do about it. While they properly recognize the authority of God over the life of the believer, they almost fatalistically resign themselves to the fact that God probably does not want to heal them and there really isn't any hope.

A Balanced Approach

Now I realize, of course, that each of the above approaches can be taken to an extreme. There are many well-meaning Christians who lean toward each of these views. And they do so in genuine faith and sincerity. However, when each approach is isolated from the others, I am convinced that it represents only an element of truth. Each is but one facet of the total picture. The three approaches are like three sides of a diamond. Someone who looks at one side only will never see the fullness of that diamond. The same is true with these perspectives in relation to human sickness and divine healing.

Physical sickness is a terrible thing to have to experience. It is true that there is a definite sense in which that sickness is ultimately a consequence of the sinful nature we inherit from Adam and Eve. But that does not mean that the individual who is ill has necessarily committed a specific sin in his or her own life which has brought about this illness. Certainly God can send sickness into our lives as a judgment for our sin, but that does not mean that all sickness is a result of the judgment of God.

In response to the faith approach, it is true that the "prayer of faith shall save the sick" (James 5:15). There are many times that God answers our prayers with a positive and complete healing. But that does not mean He is obligated to do that in every situation. Nor does the lack of healing imply that God is against us. For example, Joni Eareckson Tada is one of the finest Christian women in our country today. Yet she is a quadriplegic who is confined to a wheelchair. It is not likely that she will ever be healed of her paralysis in this lifetime. She has accepted that condition with such grace and sincerity that God has used her to speak from her wheelchair in a manner that has undoubtedly been far more significant and effective than she could ever have done under more normal circumstances.

Then there is also the truth that God is sovereign in the events of our lives and that there are times He chooses not to heal us. But that doesn't mean we should not pray for healing. You and I do not know what God's ultimate will is for our situation; therefore, we have every reason to appeal to Him in faith for healing.

Causes of Sickness

We need to understand that there are a number of causes of physical sickness. The experience of illness is not always brought about for the same reasons; it is, therefore, important for us to understand the possible reasons why we are sick if we are to understand the purpose in that sickness. Let's look now at some of those causes.

Sickness Results from Aging

Whether we like to think about it or not, the older we get the closer we come to death. Our bodies are in the process of aging every single day. We may try to camouflage that process, but it is still going on in our bodies. We can dye our hair, buy a wig, get a face-lift, or tuck our tummy. But the truth is, we are still getting older. I once heard an elderly man say, "I can see with my bifocals, my dentures work just fine, I can live with my arthritis, but I sure do miss my mind." While that may have been said in jest, it still represents the reality that aging is an ongoing process within us.

It does not matter how healthy you are right now. One day, illness will catch up with you and you will eventually die. The Bible says very clearly, "It is appointed unto men once to die" (Hebrews 9:27). Unless Christ returns in our lifetime, we all have an appointment with death. You may not like thinking about it, but it is an ever-encroaching reality that we must face. Most of us are like comedian Woody Allen, who said, "I don't mind the thought of dying so much; I just don't want to be there when it happens." But ultimately, we will.

One of the greatest men who ever lived was the prophet Elisha. He was the understudy to the prophet Elijah. When Elijah departed to heaven, the Bible says, a double portion of his spirit fell upon Elisha (*see* 2 Kings 2:9-10). As God's new prophet, Elisha was used of God to accomplish incredible miracles. On one occasion he healed the Syrian general Naaman of his leprosy, and on another occasion he raised a young boy from the dead. There can be no doubt that Elisha worked miracles by the power of God. Nevertheless, the Bible says, "Now Elisha was fallen sick of his sickness whereof he died" (2 Kings 13:14). It is highly unlikely that he died because of the judgment of God against a particular sin in his life. Rather, he died as a result of old age. Even Lazarus, whom Jesus raised from the dead, eventually died again. For the vast majority of people, death comes as a result of sickness due to aging.

Sickness Can Result from Sin

The apostle Paul affirmed this truth when he said, "For this cause many are weak and sickly among you, and many sleep" (1 Corinthians 11:30). He was writing to the Corinthian believers about various problems of sin and disobedience in their lives. "For this cause" refers to the sin which had caused many of them to suffer physical illness and had even brought about the premature death of some.

There is no doubt that sin can cause sickness. The tragic consequences of a sinful lifestyle often bring about serious illness and even premature death. The alcoholic who drinks himself into an early grave is certainly a prime example. The same is true for the excessive smoker who destroys his own respiratory system. Dr. Linus Pauling, a Nobel prize-winning chemist, has observed that every cigarette reduces a person's life expectancy by 14 minutes. That means that every pack of cigarettes takes 4.8 hours off your life. The excessive eater faces similar consequences. Many Christians who are strongly opposed to smoking and drinking are often just as guilty of excess through overeating, which can damage one's physical body. The drug addict is certainly another example of someone who is hurting himself.

The real tragedy of sickness that results from sinful habits and practices is that it destroys a person physically, mentally, and spiritually. You cannot abuse yourself and expect God to simply reverse the destructive process that you have brought about. Undoubtedly, the most serious consequence of a life of self-indulgence is the spiritual damage that takes place in a person.

It is not my purpose to specify one form of abuse as necessarily more serious than another. Rather, I am concerned that you understand that your body is the temple of the Holy Spirit of God (*see* 1 Corinthians 6:19-20). Therefore, it does make a difference what you do with your body and what you put into it. Your body belongs to God. While you and I cannot permanently forestall the aging process in our lives, we certainly have an obligation not to speed it up.

Sickness Can Come from Satan

In the story of Job we see Satan put his hand against Job to cause both calamity and physical illness in his life. While God set a limit on the extent of Satan's ability to inflict illness upon Job, He nevertheless allowed Satan to do it. The Bible says Satan went forth "from the presence of the LORD and smote Job with sore boils" (Job 2:7). Job was suffering not because of sin in his own life but because Satan had afflicted him. Now that does not mean that all sickness is a direct result of Satan's activity. But this passage makes it clear that it is possible for that to happen. In Luke 13:11-13, we read the story of a woman who cried out to Jesus and asked Him to cast out the devil within her. When He did, she was made well physically. Acts 10:38 refers to the healing ministry of Jesus and states that He healed those who were "oppressed of the devil." Even the apostle Paul referred to his physical suffering as the act of Satan "to buffet me" (2 Corinthians 12:7), referring to the fact that Satan was using that sickness to discourage him and wear him down.

Sickness Is Sometimes Allowed by God

In the lives of both Job and Paul, sickness was allowed by God in order to accomplish His greater purpose. God allowed Satan to put his hand against Job, but He also set a limit on what Satan could do and demanded that he not take Job's life. This truth brings great reassurance to us that if we are suffering as a believer, we can be sure that God will not allow us to suffer beyond the limit that He has set. It's also important to note that Job's suffering was allowed by God as a lesson to Satan himself. Most of us will never be put in that position. But in Job's case, God understood that he was such a righteous man that even his personal and physical suffering would not cause him to lose his confidence in Him.

In the apostle Paul's life, God used suffering to display His glory. In so doing, Paul stated that he was actually sharing in the "sufferings of Christ" (2 Corinthians 1:5). For Paul, this was a cause for rejoicing. He was more than willing to allow God to accomplish His purposes in his life, even if it meant personal, physical suffering.

The Solution to Sickness

As we have seen, there are many reasons why people are sick. For some people, sickness is a direct result of a sinful lifestyle. But for others, it is merely a result of the aging process. For some, sickness is an attack of Satan. But in every case, God sets sovereign limits on that suffering and overrules it for His own good purposes. If you are presently suffering from physical illness in your life, let me suggest the following steps for dealing with that sickness.

Confess and Forsake Known Sin

Examine your heart and make sure you're not suffering because of deliberate sin in your life. If you are, confess that sin to God and forsake it. If you are ill because of a destructive habit that is destroying your physical body, you may not be able to undo all of the damage that has been done; but the sooner you quit, the better. Without making a complete break from that habit, you may never know the kind of health that you could have known had you quit.

You can continue to go through the routine of life and pretend that your illness is not all that serious. But chances are that it will eventually take you. I can think of nothing more tragic than for a person to die prematurely because of a sinful habit that he or she knew was harmful but refused to give up. The psalmist put it like this: "Before I was afflicted I went astray: but now have I kept thy word" (Psalm 119:67). He acknowledged that his sinful lifestyle had led him astray and resulted in physical illness. But then he came to a point of physical repentance and returned to the Lord and resumed keeping His commandments.

The longer you indulge in sinful habits, the more you will accelerate the process of sickness and death in your own body. The sooner you turn away from those habits, the more quickly you can hope to return to health.

Pray in Faith for Your Healing

I believe Scripture clearly teaches that we can come to God by faith and claim physical healing. I do not believe that we can demand it of God in every situation. But I am convinced that we can come boldly before the throne of grace and call upon God for healing.

One of the great promises in the Word of God is found in 1 John 5:14-15, which says, "This is the confidence that we have in him, that, if we ask any thing according to his will, he heareth us: and if we know that he hear us, whatsoever we ask, we know that we have the petitions that we desired of him." This is a response of confidence in the goodness of God. There are many times in our lives when God will respond to our requests for physical healing and a restoration of health. As the aging process continues, however, we cannot expect to delay the inevitable on this side of heaven. But we can have the confidence that God does hear our prayers and delights in healing us.

The key to the balanced approach to this issue is understanding the importance of the phrase "according to his will" (1 John 5:14). It is important that we understand that healing is conditioned upon the will and purposes of God. Therefore, we must understand that there are multiple facets to this truth. When sickness results from sinful practices, that sickness may continue to have ongoing consequences in our lives even after we have repented. The drug addict who stops taking drugs cannot expect to be instantly cured of all the consequences of drug abuse. But with repentance comes the cessation of that habit, which would have caused even greater damage if it had persisted.

Another facet of truth is that when God answers the prayer of faith, He does so within the context of His will. The Bible does not say this to dampen our faith, but to balance it. I am convinced that God wants us to come to Him in faith and ask for His miraculous intervention on our behalf. But He does not guarantee healing based upon the degree of our faith. The healing response of God is conditioned upon both our faith and His will.

Trust in God to Do That Which Is Best

There is a vast difference between trusting the sovereignty of God and fatalistically resigning yourself to sickness without any hope of change. For example, if you have been told that you have cancer, you can either resign yourself to the consequences and sit there and die or you can take every possible medical procedure to help cure the cancer and pray in faith that God would heal you. I believe the latter option is the correct one.

All of us have seen people who have received their healing through prayer and medicine working hand in hand. The essence of such prayer ought to be as follows:

> Dear Lord, I know that You love me more than I love myself. I believe that Your purposes for my life are greater than my own could ever be. Therefore, I believe You will answer my prayer in the greatest way possible. I am asking You to heal me of this sickness. And I am trusting You to do what is best in my life.

When you pray like that, you will have come to a point of spiritual maturity where you are able to trust the sovereign purposes of God *and* believe that He can move miraculously in your behalf. Your petition can be made in bold confidence, but also with the attitude that you'll accept God's ultimate will as best. Then you can rest in the calm assurance that Romans 8:28 is true: "We know that all things work together for good to them that love God, to them who are the called according to his purpose."

5

How to Keep On Keeping On

We have talked a little about Job up to this point, but now we're going to take a closer look at him because there is much we can learn from him about victory in life's most difficult hours. His story is one of the most incredible accounts in Scripture. It is set in the days of the ancient patriarchs, and it reveals the cosmic spiritual struggle that goes on in heaven behind the scenes of this life.

As Job is introduced in the Bible book that bears his name, we are told that he was a man of great wealth and substance. He had seven sons and three daughters, and he was blessed with 7,000 sheep, 3,000 camels, 500 yoke of oxen, and 500 donkeys. By today's standards, Job would have been a Rockefeller or a Getty. He would have driven a Rolls Royce and lived in a mansion. He was wealthy beyond comprehension.

The Scripture also tells us that he was a righteous man who loved God, goodness, and his family. The King James text says that he "eschewed" evil, meaning that he despised it with all his heart. The Bible also emphasizes that Job's wealth was a blessing from God. Job was a man blessed of God and one who used his wealth to bring glory to God.

In the middle of Job chapter 1 we read that Satan appeared before God and complained that Job served Him only because God had so abundantly blessed him. Satan then challenged God to come against Job and predicted that if He did, Job would turn against Him. Instead, God told Satan, "Behold, all that he hath is in thy power; only upon himself put not forth thine hand" (Job 1:12). In that verse, God emphasized a great spiritual truth: Satan has no power over our lives except by the permission of God.

So in time, Satan took all of Job's possessions. Wealth could easily be lost in the ancient East, and so it was with Job. In one day, bandits stole all his sheep and cattle. His herds were devastated and his servants slaughtered. Then, before the day was over, all of his children were killed by a desert storm when the house they were in collapsed.

Trust in the Providence of God

Devastated by these personal tragedies, Job simply responded, "Naked came I out of my mother's womb, and naked shall I return thither: the LORD gave, and the LORD hath taken away; blessed be the name of the LORD" (Job 1:21). The Scripture further explains that in all that happened, Job did not sin against God with his heart.

Again Satan came before God, and the Lord pointed to Job as an example of personal integrity. But this time the devil argued that if he could touch Job's body with illness, Job would turn against God. "Skin for skin," Satan said, "yea, all that a man hath will he give for his life. But put forth thine hand now, and touch his bone and his flesh, and he will curse thee to thy face" (Job 2:4-5). But again God refused to touch His servant: "Behold, he is in thine hand; but save his life" (verse 6).

This time Satan struck Job with a terrible disease. Job came down with boils which covered his entire body from head to foot. He had not only lost what he loved most—his children—and what he valued most—his possessions—but now he lost his health as well.

As the scene opens in this section of the story, Job is sitting in a pile of ashes, pathetically scraping himself with a broken piece of pottery. He has been reduced to the trash pile of life. Can you imagine his suffering and pain? Broken and rejected, he sits there all alone.

Even Job's wife and friends could not understand his agony. His wife cried out in frustration for Job to curse God and die (Job 2:9). "Why don't you just get it over with?" is what she would have said in our terminology. "Why fight it? It's not worth it!" But Job replied, "Shall we receive good at the hand of God, and shall we not receive evil?" (verse 10). And Job's friends, who had come to console him, eventually ended up accusing him of hiding some secret sin. Their consolation turned to condemnation and criticism. Just when Job thought things could not possibly get worse, they did—his wife and friends had given up on him.

Even when all is going wrong,
God is going right.

But in all this, Job did not let his faith in God waver. In spite of his personal pain, he learned to keep on keeping on by the grace of God. And because of that faith, eventually God vindicated him and blessed him with ten more children and twice as many possessions as he had before. Job knew that he could depend on God no matter what went wrong. We too can learn how to handle life's toughest problems as we come to the realization that when all goes wrong, God is going right. He is still moving on our behalf with our greatest good as His greatest interest.

The real question for each of us to ask ourselves is, How are we doing with our problems? Has Satan ever bombarded you and gotten you down? Has he ever pulled the rug out from under your life and left you in a heap of ashes? If he has, this is no time to quit. We all get down at times. When we do get down, we get lonely and start to wallow in self-pity, feeling like nobody understands our pains and our problems.

Whenever we're down, we tend to think that we are the only ones suffering in all the world. We feel like nobody understands or cares. That is when Satan comes along and says, "Hey, nobody really loves you anyway. You're worthless. You've blown it! Why don't you just give up? You're a nobody!"

Whenever the devil tries to beat you down like that, remember Job. In spite of all his troubles and even the rejection of his wife and friends, Job hung in there with God. He put his confidence in God's personal integrity and trusted Him with his very existence.

Hang onto the Promises of God

Job's greatest source of strength was this: He believed in the promises of God. He knew in the depth of his heart that he could trust God to be true to what He had promised and bring him through his troubles. There is absolutely nothing that can occur in our lives that God has not promised to see us through.

In Psalm 121:1-2 we read, "I will lift up mine eyes unto the hills, from whence cometh my help. My help cometh from the LORD, which made heaven and earth." This makes it clear that God will be there to help us when we cannot help ourselves. He is mighty on our behalf. In the same passage we read, "He will not suffer thy foot to be moved: he that keepeth thee will not slumber" (verse 3). God never sleeps as He watches over us, and no trouble that comes our way can catch Him off guard. Once we accept Christ as our Savior, God is with us, ready to love and help us in our time of need. We have His promise on that!

In Proverbs 18:10, the Bible tells us, "The name of the LORD is a strong tower: the righteous runneth into it, and is safe." God is our refuge in times of trouble. He may not always choose to keep us *from* trouble, but He has promised to keep us *through* our trouble. There is not one difficulty or perplexity of life that God cannot help us overcome. He has promised to be our refuge from all the storms of life.

In the Bible, there are many examples used from nature to illustrate God's protection for our lives. One is that of an eagle who watches over her brood and protects them under her wings during times of storm (*see* Deuteronomy 32:11). As the rains fall and the winds blow upon that nest, the mother eagle keeps her eaglets protected by her wings. In the same manner, when the storms of life bombard us, God covers us with His protection and tells us to rest in His promises.

One of the great examples of faith in the Bible was Abraham, who believed the promises of God. The Lord called him to leave his native city of Ur in ancient Babylon and travel to that outpost of civilization called Canaan. So Abraham believed the promises of God, and with his wife and their belongings, headed for Canaan.

Abraham had no friends to welcome him into this strange new place, but he had the confidence that God went with him. And in spite of his personal struggle over the promise that he would have a son and that his seed would possess the land, Abraham persevered by faith in God's promises. Romans 4:18 explains that Abraham was one "who against hope believed in hope." In other words, when all human hope was gone, Abraham kept his hope in the Lord. He kept on keeping on because he believed the promises of God.

Rely on the Provision of God

A promise is only as good as the one who makes it. Behind every promise is a promisor who must make good his promise. The Bible tells us that God Himself is the great provider who brings His promises to fruition in our lives.

Our hope is not just in the promises of God but in the Person of God Himself. He is the one who stands behind His promises. There is an old black spiritual which says, "He's got the whole world in his hands." And indeed He does. God is the creator and sustainer of life. He is the one who spoke the world into existence. He made us; He sustains us; and He keeps us in the palm of His hand. He is also the same one who said, "I will never leave thee, nor forsake thee" (Hebrews 13:5).

*True faith will face
any disaster with the confidence
that God will see us through it.*

Job was able to endure life's calamities because he had a Provider who was greater than His provisions—God Himself. Job was not trusting in his riches; he was trusting in his God. He was not relying on his friends to see him through; he was relying on the provision of his God to meet his needs.

True faith will face any disaster with the confidence that God will see us through it. The Bible promises us, "Eye hath not seen, nor ear heard, neither have entered into the heart of man, the things which God hath prepared for them that love him" (1 Corinthians 2:9).

God knows exactly *what* we need and *when* we need it. He is the great Provider of all our needs, but He wants us to learn to trust Him to make provision for us. It is one thing to know that God can provide, but it is another thing to know that He will provide exactly what we need when we need it.

God will always
make a way out for those
who trust Him.

When I was a child, my father told me a story that taught me to persevere through life's difficulties. He told me the story of two frogs that were hopping through a barn where a farmer was milking a cow. When the farmer finished, he got up to care for one of the animals and left the bucket of milk sitting on the floor of the barn.

The two frogs came upon the bucket and wondered what was inside. One suggested that the other hop into the bucket to investigate.

"I'm not going alone," he replied.

"Very well," responded the other frog, "I'll jump in if you will."

Well, they both took a big leap and landed in the milk. At first, they were splashing around and having a great time until they realized they couldn't get out of the pail. Then, as they began to tire from swimming around, one of the frogs said, "We might as well give up. We're never going to get out of here!"

"Oh no," said the other frog. "We can't give up now. We have to keep on trying."

"Not me," said the first frog. "I've had enough. I'm going to give up." Bloop...bloop...gloop! Down he went into the milk and drowned.

The other frog kept splashing and kicking, splashing and kicking, until finally, to his amazement, the milk began to curdle, and after a while it became a plug of butter. Then the frog hopped from the top of that plug of butter and jumped out of the bucket.

My father looked at me and said, "Son, there may be times when you feel like you're drowning. You may even want to give up altogether. If you do, down you will go. Remember, son, a child of God never gives up. He keeps on kicking because he knows God is in control. And God will always make a way out for those who trust Him and never give up."

Realize the Price
Has Already Been Paid

We can learn to endure the problems of life because the price that is necessary for our deliverance has already been paid. God knew that we could never save ourselves. He also knew that we could never pay for our redemption. Therefore, He paid the price for us. You see, becoming a Christian is a free offer of God's grace, but the cost of our salvation isn't cheap. It cost God the sacrifice of His dear Son, who died for our sins that we might be set free.

In a very real sense, God paid for our salvation. I believe it is time we realized what Jesus did for us. The prophet Isaiah said, "He was wounded for our transgressions, he was bruised for our iniquities" (Isaiah 53:5). Jesus paid a price more precious than gold or jewels. He gave Himself for our salvation.

It took me several years of preaching to come to a full realization of what Christ did for me. I knew about His physical suffering. I knew that He was beaten with a whip until His back was ripped open, exposing raw flesh. I knew that He was bruised beyond recognition and nailed to a cross. I knew that He bled and died on the cross. I knew that He looked down on the angry mob with eyes filled with compassion.

But it took a work of the Holy Spirit in my heart to fully comprehend that Christ did all of that for *me*. He suffered for my sins. He died for every wrong thing I will ever do upon this earth. Not only did He die for me, but for every man, woman, and child who has ever lived.

When we try to envision Jesus on the cross, we tend to see only His *physical* suffering. But the greatest agony that day was His *spiritual* pain. As Jesus hung on the cross, God poured out our sin upon Him. Jesus took our place and suffered on our behalf. As God the Father looked down from heaven, He saw Jesus as a condemned sinner and poured out all of His divine wrath upon that sin.

In that moment God saw your sin and my sin and judged it once and for all time. Our sin was put to death in Jesus Christ. When He died on the cross, He took your place, bore your sin, and received God's judgment against that sin. He went through all of that for you because He loved you.

In that moment of condemnation and separation, Jesus cried, "My God, my God, why hast thou forsaken me?" (Matthew 27:46). It was for you and for me that He endured such punishment. But He finally triumphed over our sin and cried victoriously, "It is finished!" (John 19:30). In that moment, our redemption was sealed.

I don't know about you, but I will never give up because I don't want my Savior to have died in vain. He paid for my redemption, and I'm not going to let Satan rob me of the joy of my salvation. I'm not going to let him discourage or defeat me because my Lord went through too much for me. He died that I might live.

Keep Your Eyes on the Prize

The Bible is filled with accounts of people who kept on by keeping their eyes on their ultimate destination. They were able to persevere because they never lost sight of the goal. The apostle Paul said, "I press toward the mark for the prize of the high calling of God in Christ Jesus" (Philippians 3:14). You and I have a destiny with Christ in heaven. We are not living just for ourselves or the pleasures of this life, but we are living with heaven in view.

Job understood that his ultimate destiny was not the ashes or even the grave. Despite all his troubles, he said, "I know that my redeemer liveth, and that he shall stand at the latter day upon the earth: And though after my skin worms destroy this body, yet in my flesh shall I see God" (Job 19:25-26).

Job never lost sight of the prize of eternal life. After all that he had suffered, he was still convinced that God was alive, that he belonged to Him, and that one day God would resurrect his mortal body to stand again upon the earth. That is what real faith is all about. It is the personal belief that we are destined for the resurrection. Whatever goes wrong here will be corrected there.

It was Job's faith in the prize of God's provision that kept him going during his toughest hours. And that is the same kind of faith that you and I need to face our most difficult trials as well. You may feel a lot like Job. You may be broken, devastated, and deserted, but God has not forsaken you. He is going to deliver you. Even when family and friends reject us, God's love still accepts us just as we are so that He can make us into what we ought to be.

If God loved you enough to send His Son to die for your sins, He loves you enough to get you through your problems and troubles. Don't give up! The price has been paid, and the prize awaits.

I leave you with these final words from Job—the testimony of one who had seen the fires of trouble and kept on keeping on. He said, "Thou shalt forget thy misery, and remember it as waters that pass away" (Job 11:16).

6

Jesus
Cares for You

*N*ot long ago I received a telephone call from a woman in her mid-thirties who had recently been divorced. She was sobbing on the other end of the phone as she tried to tell me of the heartbreaking circumstances she was going through. Her husband had left her for another woman. Then after the divorce, her teenage daughter had run away from home.

This young mother proceeded to tell me how she had searched all over America for her daughter. She spent hundreds of dollars on telephone calls and finally located her daughter in a distant city. She bought an airplane ticket at great expense and flew to the city to bring her daughter home. When she finally found her, the mother threw her arms around her, told her she loved her, and asked her to come home.

Bitter from the pain of her parents' divorce, the girl pushed her mother away. "I don't love you or Dad," she snapped harshly. "And I never want to see you again. Get out of my life and leave me alone."

The mother wept as she said, "Pastor, I don't know if I can go on. Nobody loves me; nobody wants me; nobody cares what happens to me now."

It may be that you are reading this today and you feel very much like she felt. Perhaps you feel that nobody loves or cares about you. If so, I want to share with you what I shared with that young mother that day. I believe with all my heart that Jesus loves you and cares about you more than you could ever know. No matter what mistakes you have made or what kind of mess you may be in, He still loves you.

The love of Christ is beyond measure. It cannot be compared to degrees of human love. To illustrate His compassion for us, Jesus compared His love to that of a shepherd who would leave 99 sheep in the fold and risk all to search for one sheep that was lost. In the parable of the lost sheep (Luke 15:3-7), Jesus told of the seeking shepherd who pursued that one sheep until he rescued it and carried it home on his shoulders rejoicing.

*The love of Christ
is beyond measure. It cannot
be compared to degrees
of human love.*

Paralleling the story of the lost sheep to that of lost humanity, Jesus said, "I say unto you, that likewise joy shall be in heaven over one sinner that repenteth, more than over ninety and nine just persons, which need no repentance" (verse 7). What a beautiful picture our Lord painted with His words! In this great analogy, He expressed how much He cares for us.

He Knows Us Individually

I have often wondered how a shepherd could know that one specific sheep was missing from the fold. There is no indication in the story that he had to be told the sheep was missing. No undershepherd announced it to him. Rather, our Lord indicated that the shepherd knew each sheep individually; therefore, he knew which one was missing. He didn't have to keep a running count to know one was missing, and He knew *which* one was missing.

With this analogy, Jesus reminds us that He knows each one of us individually. You are not just a number in the mind of God; you are a specific person of individual significance to the Lord. God cares about you individually and personally. Although Christ came to save the masses of humanity and die for the whole world, He also came to die for you specifically. And regardless of all your problems, mistakes, and errors, God loves you personally. He knows your name and your needs, and He is prepared to meet the deepest longings of your heart.

I once read a story of a census taker who knocked on the door of a home. When the woman of the house answered the door, the census taker asked her a series of questions. Finally, he asked, "What is the number of your children?" The woman thought for a moment, then said, "I don't understand what you mean." The census taker replied, "I need to know the number of your children."

"You must be mistaken," the woman responded. "Sir, my children don't have numbers; they have names!"

That is how God treats His children. He calls us all by name. You will never read in the Bible that God called somebody, "Hey, you." He always called people by their names—Adam, Abraham, Jacob, Moses, Samuel, and Mary. God knows us individually. The Bible tells us that He even knows the number of hairs we have on our heads (*see* Luke 12:7).

Becoming a Christian is also an individual matter. You are not a Christian just because your parents are Christians. God doesn't have any grandchildren. He accepts us one by one. The fact that your father or mother may be Christians is irrelevant to the matter of whether you are a true believer yourself.

All too often people think they are Christians because they attend a certain church or belong to a particular denomination. Jesus Himself made it clear that not all who call Him Lord are truly saved (*see* Matthew 7:21-23). He even went so far as to tell Nicodemus, a ruler of the Jews, that he must be born again (John 3:5-7). Our Lord did not commend the ruler's righteous life and urge him to continue on with his good works. Rather, Jesus made it clear to him that his works could not save him apart from spiritual rebirth.

Just as Christ knows us individually, so also must we come to know Him individually and personally. He is not just a religious symbol; He is a real person who can be known in an intimate and personal way. I remember once hearing a little girl say the Lord's Prayer incorrectly. She got the words wrong, but she got the idea right when she said, "Our Father which art in heaven, how does He know my name?"

No matter how impersonal the modern world may seem, God is still a personal God seeking us on an individual basis and calling us to abide under His care.

He Seeks Us Personally

I have always been impressed by the simple fact that the shepherd in the parable of the lost sheep went seeking the lost animal personally. He didn't send an assistant or delegate the responsibility to a committee. He went himself to find the sheep. He didn't even send another shepherd to search first; he went himself.

Whenever I try to comprehend the simple truth that Christ left heaven for me personally, I am absolutely astounded. Why would the King of Creation leave His throne and be born in a manger to pursue one of His creatures? What advantage was it to Him? Why should He leave the glory of heaven to risk all on the cross for me? Yet the greatest fact of history is that Jesus Christ did exactly that. He who had dominion over all powers subjugated Himself to human flesh. He could have sent an angel, but He came in person that starry Bethlehem night to claim us for Himself. Concerning that event, someone has said,

> That night when in the Judean skies
> The mystic star dispensed its light,
> A blind man moved in his sleep—
> And dreamed that he had sight!
>
> That night when shepherds heard the song
> Of hosts angelic choiring near;
> A deaf man stirred in slumber's spell—
> And dreamed that he could hear!
>
> That night when in the cattle stall
> Slept child and mother cheek by jowl,
> A cripple turned his twisted limbs—
> And dreamed that he was whole!
>
> That night when o'er the newborn babe
> The tender Mary rose to lean,
> A loathsome leper smiled in sleep—
> And dreamed that he was clean!
>
> That night when to the mother's heart
> The little King was held secure,
> A harlot slept a happy sleep—
> And dreamed that she was pure!
>
> That night when in the manger lay
> The sanctified who came to save,
> A man moved in the sleep of death—
> And dreamed there was no grave.

> Author Unknown

No one else could have accomplished our redemption. Only the sinless Son of God could lay down His life as an acceptable sacrifice for our sins. Only His blood could wash away our iniquity and set us free from the penalty of condemnation that we deserved.

In your moments of greatest doubt or personal struggle, you might question whether or not God really loves you. When you find yourself struggling like that, remind yourself that God loved you so much that He sent His Son to die for you personally. Whenever a person lays down his life for someone else, he has done all he could do to prove his love for that person.

When I think of those who gave their lives in Vietnam, Korea, or during World War II, I am amazed at their love and devotion. They gave all they had that we might be free. In a very real sense, they gave their lives for us. Yet some have questioned their integrity and commitment, especially those who fought in Vietnam. I find that hard to understand. Whenever someone lays down his or her life for others, he or she has given the ultimate measure of his or her devotion.

By the same token, how can anyone question the love of Christ? How can we dare suggest that He does not care for us when He gave His life for us on the cross? He did not die as a martyr or a victim. He died willingly and deliberately in our place. He was not murdered; He laid down His life intentionally. He was not caught in an inescapable series of events; He came into this world to die for our sins and then to triumph over them by His resurrection. The crowd may have called for His crucifixion. The governor may have permitted it. The priests may have demanded it. But Jesus Christ laid down His own life deliberately on our behalf.

He Carries Our Burdens

In our Lord's parable about the lost sheep, we notice that the shepherd tenderly picked up the sheep and carried it upon his shoulders. He could have reprimanded the sheep and ordered it to go home; instead, he picked it up and carried it home.

We have a little brown poodle at home named Ginger. Little Ginger is like a member of our family. She even has her own room in our basement. When we come home and open the door of her room, she comes bounding out and jumps excitedly all over us. We pick her up and hug her because she is a dear little friend.

It is often said that a dog is a man's best friend. I can see why. Ginger, like other dogs, can't talk back to us. She has never made an ugly remark or an unkind comment to us. She is just a source of unconditional acceptance and joy to all of our family.

I can imagine the joy of that little sheep when he was found by the shepherd. I can picture him, lost, alone, cold, and afraid. I can see him struggling to stay afoot on the craggy mountain ledges. I can see the panic in his eyes as he hears the howling wolves in the distance.

What's strange about sheep is that when they get lost, they become helpless and cannot find their way. They must be sought, or they could be forever lost. In the beauty of our Lord's parable, the shepherd went searching for the sheep and called it to himself.

Jesus said that sheep respond only to the voice of their shepherd, who calls them all by name (John 10:3). "The sheep follow him," our Lord explained, "for they know his voice" (John 10:4). He then announced, "I am the good shepherd: the good shepherd giveth his life for the sheep" (John 10:11). He also explained that He knows His sheep, calls His sheep, and gives His life for His sheep. "My sheep hear my voice, and I know them, and they follow me: and I give unto them eternal life; and they shall never perish, neither shall any man pluck them out of my hand" (John 10:27-28).

Can't you just picture this helpless little lost sheep? Suddenly, he hears the shepherd's voice. *That's my shepherd*, he thinks. Animals do think, you know. Then he bleats out his cry for help. The shepherd hears that little bleat and comes and takes the sheep in his arms. The shepherd holds him close and calms his fears and then hoists him onto his shoulders and carries him home.

Our Lord could not have chosen a more appropriate picture to illustrate His love for us. What more vivid way could He tell us to trust Him to carry our burdens and bring us safely to heaven? "I will take you just as you are," is what He is implying in this parable. "I will love you and forgive you." Then He puts us on His shoulders and carries us home.

He Keeps Us Safe

In the parable of the lost sheep, Jesus said that the shepherd took the sheep *home* to the fold. God does not find us in order to lose us. He does not forgive us and then condemn us. As we have already seen, He gives us *eternal* life. The unique quality of that spiritual life is that it lasts forever. It is not eternal one moment and then temporal the next. It lasts forever, and those who have it live forever.

Once Christ puts you on His shoulder, He will never let you down.

When Christ claims us for Himself, He brings us into a permanent and eternal relationship with Himself. Once He puts you on His shoulder, He will never let you down. Once you are safe within His fold, you will never be lost again. God's love is unconditional. It is based upon His grace and not our merits. His is not a conditional love that demands that we meet His criteria in order to remain in His fold.

If our security depended on our ability not to fail, we would all be lost. Fortunately, our security depends upon His power to save us and sustain us. We can persevere because His Spirit is at work in us.

The gospel, in a nutshell, is stated in John 3:16: "For God so loved the world, that he gave his only begotten Son, that whosoever believeth in him should not perish, but have everlasting life." "Everlasting" is a powerful word. The dictionary describes it as that which remains for all time. The biblical term is synonymous with the word "eternal." In other words, the salvation which Christ offers us is that which places us safely, securely, and permanently in heaven forever.

This salvation is God's free gift to mankind. He offers it willingly and freely to all who will repent and take it by faith. That is why Jesus said there is joy in heaven "over one sinner that repenteth" (Luke 15:7). Nine hundred and sixty-nine times, the Bible calls us to repent. It is the message of the prophets, of John the Baptist, of Jesus, and of the apostles.

In the New Testament, *repent* means to "change your mind" (Greek, *metanoeō*), and in the Old Testament, it means to "turn" or "change your direction" (Hebrew, *shub*). Thus, the full biblical picture of repentance is a change of mind about your sin which results in a change of direction in your life.

Christ, our Shepherd, has left the fold of heaven to seek us among the rocks of this life. When He finds us, He saves us because we cannot save ourselves. He rescues us from destruction and carries us home to heaven.

When we forsake all human effort to save ourselves and instead cast ourselves on His mercy, we will always find Him ready to receive us. It doesn't matter how badly you may have failed, He has succeeded in securing your redemption. It doesn't matter what you may have done wrong; He has done right for you. It doesn't matter who has rejected you; He will accept you, for He is the gentle Shepherd who cares for you!

Part 3

Deliverance from Your Temptations

7

Dare to Tackle Temptation

*F*rom the day we are born until we leave this physical world, we have a constant companion called temptation. Whether or not we sense its presence, temptation is always there stalking us like a lion stalking his prey. No matter how long you have walked with God, temptation is always a potential danger in your life.

But I have good news for you. God understands the pressure of our temptations and He has made provision for our escape. The Bible says, "There hath no temptation taken you but such as is common to man: but God is faithful, who will not suffer you to be tempted above that ye are able; but will with the temptation also make a way to escape, that ye may be able to bear it" (1 Corinthians 10:13).

Isn't that a marvelous thought! God knows us so well that He not only knows us personally, but He also knows all the trials and struggles we are going to face in life. That is why He gave us His Word—to help us understand the temptations we would face and to help us gain victory over them.

I recall counseling a man in his mid-fifties. He admitted a particularly difficult sin in his life and said, "Pastor, will this temptation ever go away?"

"Not on this side of heaven," I replied.

"Do you mean that I'm always going to have to fight this in order to defeat it?" he asked.

"Yes," I said, "in all likelihood, you will always have to deny its claim on your life."

Not all temptation works like that. Sometimes it is little more than a fleeting glance or thought. Other times, the temptation is lodged deep within our own depravity. Still other times it is a reflection of our own personal weakness. Whatever the case, God can help us overcome it.

The word "tempt" (Greek, *peirazō*) has a twofold meaning in the New Testament. In a positive sense, it means "to test," "try," or "prove." In a negative sense, it means "to ensnare" or "lead astray." Thus, while the devil attempts to ensnare us through temptation, God often uses such trials to let us prove and strengthen our faith in Him.

What Is Temptation?

If I am going to face temptation all my life, then I had better understand what it is and how it works. Only in so doing can I ever hope to control it and defeat it. Thus we must begin by discovering where temptation comes from and clearly defining it in our minds.

Many people blame temptation on God. They act as though their enticement to sin comes from Him. I have actually had people ask me, "Why did God tempt me to sin?" or, "Why did God bring this temptation into my life?"

The Bible clearly tells us that God is not the author of sin. In James 1:13 we read, "Let no man say when he is tempted, I am tempted of God: for God cannot be tempted with evil, neither tempteth he any man."

This scripture makes it clear that God is not the creator of temptation. He is not the source of our enticement to do wrong. To the contrary, He wants to live with us in perfect peace and harmony. God loves us and wants the very best for us. While He may allow us to be tempted, He is not the source of that temptation.

There are two major sources of temptation: one is internal, and the other is external. Internal temptation is described in James 1:14: "Every man is tempted, when he is drawn away of his own lust, and enticed." Sometimes our struggle with temptation is an internal battle that we attempt to blame on someone other than ourselves.

Psychologists call this "projection." Often we project upon others the blame for problems that we really make for ourselves. Edwin Sabin says it this way in the poem "Myself":

> An enemy I had whose face
>   I stoutly strove to know,
> For hard he dogged my steps, unseen,
>   Wherever I might go.
>
> My plans he balked, my aims he foiled,
>   He blocked my onward way.
> When for some lofty goal I toiled,
>   He grimly said me nay.
>
> "Come forth!" I cried, "Lay bare thy guise!
>   Thy features I would see,"
> But always to my straining eyes
>   He dwelt in mystery.
>
> One night I seized and held him fast,
>   The veil from him did draw,
> I gazed upon his face at last...
>   And lo! Myself I saw.

But other times the conflict is external, and we are tempted by Satan himself. When God created Adam and Eve, He placed them in the Garden of Eden. There, it was heaven on earth—the garden was full of the love and protection of Almighty God. But when Satan entered the scene in the form of the serpent, he tempted Adam and Eve by telling them that if they ate of the forbidden fruit, they would be as gods themselves. They yielded to that temptation, and humankind has had to suffer the consequences ever since. In all that took place in the Garden, one thing was clear: Satan was the author of temptation. He still is, and he has used it since that day to try to destroy the children of God.

Satan's Desperate Attempts

With that in mind, let us think about what temptation really is. After all, if we are going to overcome it we must be able to identify it. It's difficult to win a war without understanding the nature of your enemy's weapon. Temptation is Satan's *attempt* to get you to commit an act of sin. Notice I said *attempt*. The whole aim and purpose of temptation is to cause you to violate God's laws and principles. Just as it is the nature of a bird to fly or a dog to bark, it is the nature of Satan to try to get you to sin.

Temptation itself is not a sin.
Yielding to temptation is the sin.

Think of the predicament Satan is in with regard to your life. If you have committed your life to Christ, he has lost your soul. He once had you twisted around his finger, and now you have escaped his dominating control. You found a better way, and took it. You discovered the avenue of escape which led to Christ, and through repentance and faith you fled to Him. Now your life belongs to God, and Satan has lost you forever.

Unfortunately, this does not mean that Satan has given up on you. Now that he has lost you, he is likely to do all he can to neutralize your faith and testimony by bombarding you with temptation. The only thing he can do to you now is to try to trip you up. He was the ruler of your life until you came to Christ by faith. Now, Christ is your Lord and Satan is rejected. God has entered your life, and that makes all the difference. He has regenerated your heart and filled your life with His Holy Spirit. All hope of damning your soul has been lost, and Satan knows it!

You and I are free in Christ. We have been redeemed by His blood and released from the bondage of sin. The condemnation of guilt has been canceled, and we have been set free. We have been granted pardon, and we have been given a brand-new life in Christ.

Satan's only remaining tactic is to target your weaknesses and try to tempt you to sin. In so doing, he hopes to bring guilt and defeat into your life so that you will stop trying to be a witness for Christ.

Remember that temptation itself is not sin. *Yielding* to temptation is the sin. Don't let Satan put you on a guilt trip because thoughts of temptation enter your mind. Jesus Himself was tempted yet never sinned (*see* Hebrews 4:15). Temptation is a real, and often daily, experience that every believer must learn how to handle. But temptation itself is not a sin. It is the lure that Satan uses to try to get us to sin.

Temptation is the enticement to sin. It may be triggered by external stimuli, but it comes to fruition in our minds. It is our own lusts and desires that drive us toward sinning. Therefore, we must learn to deal with and control these desires if we are going to overcome temptation.

Where Does the Battle Begin?

Temptation may be triggered by a physical urge or desire, but it is essentially a mental process. The Bible describes the threefold nature of temptation as 1) "the lust of the flesh," 2) "the lust of the eyes," and 3) "the pride of life" (1 John 2:16). This description makes it clear that the physical and mental aspects of temptation are closely interrelated.

The Mind

Temptation begins in the mind. It may germinate from the physical, but it comes to full fruition in one's mind. Rarely do people jump into sin spontaneously. Most of the time, people fall into sin because they spent a great deal of time thinking about it.

Once your mind focuses and dwells upon a particular temptation, you are in real danger of going all the way. You may start trying to talk yourself out of it. You may even argue and debate with yourself. But it is difficult to argue yourself out of a desire.

The mind is the gate through which everything enters our lives. That is why we are warned in Scripture to guard ("keep") our minds and to "think" on those things which will strengthen us spiritually (Philippians 4:7-8). This is especially true today; Satan has so infiltrated our society that our world is filled with pictures, movies, magazines, and television programs which can quickly and easily lead us astray from the very things we believe.

The Bible reminds us, "As [a man] thinketh in his heart, so is he" (Proverbs 23:7). The mind is like a computer. It can be programmed with spiritual truth or with evil thoughts. The choice is really up to you. You can choose to think on good, wholesome, positive, and virtuous things, or you can fill your mind with sinful thoughts.

Two of the aspects of temptation, "lust of the eyes" and the "pride of life," involve the mind. It is in our minds that we talk to ourselves, and in some cases, even argue with ourselves.

A recent study by a noted psychologist stated that the average American speaks between 150 to 200 words a minute. I think the 150 is a Georgian, and the 200 is a New Yorker! That study also indicated that our minds think at the rate of 1,300 words a minute. That means you can think faster than you can verbalize those thoughts into words. That is why we must learn to discipline our minds to focus on the things of God.

The Body

The "lust of the flesh" is the desire for physical gratification. This can lead to such sinful indulgences as overeating, excessive drinking, or illicit sex. As long as we live inside a physical body, we are going to be tempted to sin with that body and to sin against that body. In fact, the body is the believer's major spiritual battleground. That is why the apostle Paul urged his readers to present their bodies as a "living sacrifice" to God (Romans 12:1).

The body is where the battle begins. It cries out for satisfaction and indulgence. But giving heed to that cry often drives people to destruction. The alcoholic who keeps on drinking is headed to an early grave. The drug addict who keeps popping pills or smoking dope is slowly but surely destroying himself. The adulterer or adulteress who continually pursues an illicit relationship is gambling with life itself.

We live in a society of instant gratification. It is very difficult for most of us to wait patiently for anything. We want it all, and we want it now! When we can't afford our desires, we just charge them up on a credit card. Ours is a society that has seen it all and done it all. Yet, most people are still restlessly unhappy. They frantically search for peace, only to have it elude them at every turn. They keep trying to find happiness in thrills that leave them cold and empty inside.

The body is a wonderful machine when it is properly cared for and used. God has designed us so that every aspect of the human anatomy functions to the fullest potential for our physical well-being. The tragedy is that some people spend a lifetime, often a short one, destroying what He has made.

The ultimate problem with temptation is that it will always hit you at the weakest point of your strongest desire. It is not necessarily the desires themselves that are wrong, but the temptation to fulfill those desires in a wrong way.

The desire for food is not a reason to gorge oneself. The desire for sexual fulfillment is not an excuse for sexual permissiveness. God has ordained that sexual satisfaction come from the bond of marriage. But Satan often tempts people to fulfill their desires in some other manner outside that bond.

You may desire praise, admiration, success, education, acceptance, or a thousand other different things. The desire may vary, but the pattern is always the same: Temptation always hits your strongest desire at your weakest point. Therefore, you must be honest with yourself by identifying and acknowledging that desire so that you can guard against it when temptation comes.

How Can I Overcome Temptation?

It is not enough to know what temptation is, where it comes from, and how it works. If you ever hope to conquer it, you must begin to take specific and forceful steps of action to confront and deny it.

Expect It

No matter how spiritual you may think you are, temptation can easily come when you least expect it. When you think your life is all it ought to be, you are in greater danger of falling than when you know you're in trouble. That is why the Bible reminds us, "Wherefore let him that thinketh he standeth take heed lest he fall" (1 Corinthians 10:12).

The method, mode, and nature of temptation may change, but it is still temptation. For example, you may not be as easily tempted by the sins of the flesh as you once were, but you may be more susceptible than ever to the sins of pride, arrogance, and self-righteousness. Don't overestimate yourself and underestimate temptation. Be prepared to deal with it at every turn. The Bible tells us that our Lord was "in all points tempted like as we are" (Hebrews 4:15). If He faced temptation, you and I can be certain that we will face it, too.

Don't Panic

You don't have to fear temptation. Just because it comes into your life doesn't mean you have to be defeated by it. Some people panic in advance. *If I'm tempted like that I know I'll give in,* they rationalize to themselves. Let me set you at ease. You will be tempted, but you don't have to give in to it. The Bible promises to us, "Greater is he that is in you, than he that is in the world" (1 John 4:4).

The apostle Paul affirmed that truth to the church at Corinth as well. He made two promises that are essential to overcoming temptation. First, he wrote, "There hath no temptation taken you but such as is common to man" (1 Corinthians 10:13). That means you are not alone in your

*You will face temptation,
but you don't have to give in to it.*

struggle with temptation. You are not the only one being tempted. Such temptation is common to human experience. Second, Paul said, "But God is faithful, who will not suffer you to be tempted above that ye are able" (verse 13). To rephrase that promise in modern English, he said that God will not allow us to be tempted beyond the point of our ability to resist. If you find yourself giving in to temptation, perhaps you need to face the fact that you are the problem, not the temptation.

"But you just wouldn't believe what I have to face every day," someone will object. May I remind you that God has said your temptation is common to all men and that others have learned to resist it? Second, may I remind you again that God said you can endure it because He has set a limit on it? Finally, remember that there is always a "way to escape" if you will only take it!

Identify It

Learn to identify the kind of temptation with which you are faced. Are you jealous by nature? Then identify your jealousy as a weakness which is prone to temptation. Do you tend to lose your temper easily? Then identify anger as a potential area of temptation.

Your area of temptation could be lust, frustration, depression, self-pity, or any one of a hundred things. Whatever it is, face up to it and plan to deal with it. Search the Word of God and see what He has to say about it. Then tackle it head-on.

Several years ago I visited a lady in the hospital who was a hypochondriac. She was always "sick" from some psychosomatic illness. She was constantly in and out of the hospital. When I asked the doctor what was wrong, he would just say, "Oh, nothing really; it's all in her head!"

I even recall visiting her at home one time when she had hundreds of pills strewn on a table. She was reading feverishly in a large black book, which I assumed was the Bible. To my dismay, I discovered it was the *Home Medical Guide,* and she was doctoring herself according to all the symptoms she thought she had. That can be dangerous as well as foolish. But that is how some people deal with temptation. They try a little of this and some of that, and hope it will go away. That simply doesn't work. But if you are willing to be honest with yourself, God will show you precisely your area of weakness.

Deny It

Ultimately the matter of overcoming temptation comes down to a decision. You must decide in your heart that you will resist temptation by the power of God. You may have yielded to it in the past, but now you determine never again to do so. Usually the people who don't overcome temptation don't really want to overcome it.

I once heard a story about a woman who was a compulsive spender. She had just bought another new dress, and her husband demanded to know why she had done so.

"Well, I guess the devil made me do it," she suggested.

"Why do you say that?" he asked.

"When I put it on, I could hear this voice telling me how good I looked in it and that I ought to buy it," she added.

"If you thought it was the devil," her husband responded, "why didn't you say 'get behind me, Satan'?"

"I did," she said with a twinkle in her eye, "but he said it looked good from back there, too!"

Most of us are just like her. We have already made up our minds that we want something regardless of the consequences. That decision can be disastrous.

Prepare for It

Since we already know that temptation comes to all of us, we need to learn to be ready for it. We tell our teenagers that if someone ever offers them drugs or tempts them to do wrong, "Just say no!" But we seldom make the same preparation ourselves. What will you say if someone asks you to bend the law in a business deal? What will you say if you are ever approached by a prostitute? What will you do if the opportunity comes to get even with your worst enemy? Will you "just say no"?

I believe that many Christians fall into temptation because they think it could never happen to them. Therefore, they are not prepared to deal with it when it does come. Think ahead. You don't have to go out looking for trouble. It will usually find you soon enough. But you had better be prepared to say no when it comes.

Deal with It

Some time ago I visited the U.S. Naval Air Base in Pensacola, Florida, where I was privileged to see an F-18 fighter plane. I was fascinated as the pilot showed me around it. It was specially equipped to detect enemy aircraft up to 100 miles away. It was a magnificent machine. "Many of its details are classified information," said the pilot. "But I can tell you this much: No enemy can ever take this airplane by surprise!"

The Holy Spirit helps us to detect temptation before it snares us.

You and I, as God's children, have the same kind of detection device. The Holy Spirit dwells within us, and He enables us to develop the sensitivity to detect temptation before it ensnares us. He convicts us of the difference between sin and righteousness and urges us to deal drastically with sin before it deals with us.

"What if you really did spot an enemy plane at 100 miles?" I asked the pilot.

"When the plane gets to within 50 miles, we would fire a missile and destroy it instantly!" he answered confidently.

That is exactly what you need to do when you recognize temptation coming your way. Identify it and deal with it immediately. The best method is to get away from the source of temptation and stay away from it.

There were once two young boys who took a shortcut through a cow pasture on their way to school. Unfortunately, there was an old bull in the pasture who became angry because they had invaded his turf. He suddenly charged toward the boys, snorting and stomping as he came. As the boys turned to run, one said to the other, "We need to stop and pray about this."

The other boy replied, "I've got a better idea. Let's run and pray!"

That is the best advice you could ever heed in regard to temptation. Don't stand around thinking about it. Run and pray!

8

How to Master Your Mind

*T*he mind is a marvelous instrument. It operates like a personalized computer, filled with millions of bits of information. Virtually every action we commit is triggered by our mind. That is why the mind is the major battleground against temptation. The Bible says, "As [a man] thinketh in his heart, so is he" (Proverbs 23:7).

Everything that we think about can potentially affect our behavior for good or evil. That's why the mind is so crucial to proper behavior. A person who dwells on negative thoughts will become negative and pessimistic. A person who focuses his or her attention on rotten thoughts will begin to act rotten. By contrast, if we fill our minds with good and wholesome things, we will begin doing good things.

Recent psychological studies have shown the interrelation between thinking and behavior. We do what we think about, and what we think about, we do. If we are willing to let God cleanse our mind and fill it with wholesome thoughts, the results will be apparent in every area of our life. But if we are unwilling to submit our thought life to Him, we will continue to be shackled by guilt and by powerful, destructive habits. Temptation will overwhelm us because we are not armed against it. So, before looking more closely at these serious problems in the life of the believer, let's see what God's Word has to say about handling thoughts and mastering the mind.

The apostle Paul put it this way:

> I beseech you therefore, brethren, by the mercies of God, that ye present your bodies a living sacrifice, holy, acceptable unto God, which is your reasonable service. And be not conformed to this world but be ye transformed by the renewing of your mind, that ye may prove what is that good, and acceptable, and perfect, will of God (Romans 12:1-2).

This familiar text is at once both profound and simple. The keys to Christian living are to present your body and renew your mind. "But how do I do it?" you ask. Let's take a look at the marvelous truth in this passage.

Renewal Begins Within

The phrase "present your bodies" means that believers are to *yield* their bodies to Christ. The word "present" is a technical term in the Greek text meaning "to present for sacrifice." The believer is to dedicate himself to God in a deliberate and intentional manner, just as one would dedicate a sacrifice to God. In fact, Paul goes on to say that such an act of dedication is our "reasonable service."

The word "reasonable" (Greek, *logikos)* means "rational" or "logical." Thus, the only logical step for believers to take is to present or dedicate themselves to the service of God. Thus, the use of our bodies is characterized by conscious, intelligent, and consecrated devotion to the service of God.

Before you can mature in your walk with God, you must face the fact that your body belongs to God. Christ died for your sins and His blood has redeemed you from the clutches of Satan. Thus, it does matter what you do with your body, because it is now not your own—it is God's.

The second aspect of this text refers to the "renewing of your mind." This is the process by which we are transformed from the world and into the image of Christ. The negative command "be not conformed" literally means "do not be formed or molded" to this world. The Phillips translation, "don't let the world around you squeeze you into its own mold," is exactly correct.

The term "transformed" (Greek, *metamorphousthe)* comes from the same root word as *metamorphosis,* meaning an inward change that results in an outward transformation. When a sluggish old caterpillar goes through metamorphosis, it is transformed into a beautiful, brightly colored butterfly. It has been changed.

This renewing of the mind is directly related to the new birth, which brings regeneration to the soul. When we are born again, we begin to think differently because we have had our spiritual sight illuminated by God. Therefore, the moral quality of our reason and activity is dramatically transformed by the power of God.

"This is fine," you say, "but how can I experience it?"

Wrong Thought Patterns

In this day of confusion and turmoil, people want to know how to find inner peace and strength. They are searching for a reality upon which to build their lives. In counseling with others, I have observed four basic thought patterns that are adversely affecting people today.

Thoughts of Immorality

This may seem like a broad category, but it isn't. Almost every area of our society is permeated with immorality. Newspapers, magazines, movies, and television programs are saturated with an emphasis on the immoral. Temptation virtually leaps off the page into the mind. The battle for the mind and the subsequent battle for the body are being waged within every one of us.

Time and time again, I am asked, "Pastor, how can I keep my mind clean in a dirty world?" This question is being asked by good people who really care about their families and their relationship with God. The temptation to get caught up in immoral behavior is not a battle which affects only dirty-minded people. It can affect us all.

Jesus said that if we lust after someone in our hearts, we are as guilty of adultery as if we had actually committed it (*see* Matthew 5:28). Obviously, the act itself is more serious in its consequences than is the thought. But actions begin as thoughts in the mind. That is why the attitudes and intentions of the heart are viewed so seriously by God. If we can learn to deny thoughts of lust, we can control our actions toward the opposite sex.

The Bible makes it clear that thoughts of temptation are one of the realities of life. They are going to come into your mind as long as you are living on planet earth in a physical body of human flesh. Remember, though, the ultimate problem is not in the temptation, but in yielding to it. D.L. Moody said it this way: "You can't keep a bird from flying over your head, but you sure can keep it from nesting in your hair!"

Some will object, arguing that they are free adults who can do what they want to do without doing wrong. I have heard people insist that they could read pornographic magazines, attend certain R-rated movies, or watch questionable cable television channels without being enticed into sin. Horsefeathers! That may sound acceptable to some, but it is nothing more than playing with fire.

Remember that sin is a process that begins in the mind. The entertainment of sinful thoughts feeds sinful attitudes in the heart and leads to sinful action and behavior in our lives. As someone once wrote,

Sow a thought, reap an act;
Sow an act, reap a habit;
Sow a habit, reap a character;
Sow a character, reap a destiny.

I think of David, the mighty warrior-king of Israel, who accidentally saw a woman bathing herself as he walked on the roof of his palace. The Bible says that David "saw a woman washing herself; and the woman was very beautiful to look upon. And David sent and enquired after the woman" (2 Samuel 11:2-3).

What are you feeding your mind? Your thoughts will determine your behavior.

Notice the progression of David's sin. First, he saw her, then he gazed upon her, and finally he sought her out. Had he dealt with this sinful progression at any point, he could have stopped the process. Instead, he fostered the process by continuing to look. His curiosity and passion were aroused. He sent to find out her identity. This implicated others in his sinful desire. Eventually he spoke with her and clearly revealed his interest and intentions. Immorality begins in the mind; it is a thought long before it is an action.

Thoughts of Trouble

Some of us battle with negative and destructive thoughts. We imagine trouble even when it doesn't exist. When we let our minds become filled with all sorts of negative thinking, we become pessimistic about everything in life. If the kids are late coming home, we imagine that they have all been in an accident or that they have been up to no good. If the boss is grouchy at work one day, we toss and turn all that night thinking about the possibility of being fired in the morning.

Our Lord dealt with this problem when He said, "Take therefore no thought for the morrow: for the morrow shall take thought for the things of itself" (Matthew 6:34). To "take thought" means to "worry" or "be anxious." Therefore, Jesus was telling His disciples not to worry about tomorrow because God would take care of them.

Worry overburdens us with the cares of a day which has not yet arrived.

We often fill our minds with worry about food, drink, clothes, job, security, and the future. Our Lord reminds us that He will care for all these things and that we need not bother ourselves with worrying about them. If we cannot trust Him to meet our needs day by day, we will never be able to enjoy each new day. That is why He added the statement, "Sufficient unto the day is the evil thereof" (Matthew 6:34). Jesus was saying that each day has enough trouble of its own without spoiling it by worrying about tomorrow.

The English word "worry" comes from an Anglo-Saxon term meaning "to strangle." When you worry, you strangle yourself. You strangle your spirit, mind, and soul with the anxieties of life. Worry keeps us from enjoying the blessings we have. It takes us beyond our immediate cares and overburdens us with the cares of a day which has not yet arrived.

Worry is an unrighteous imagination. It means taking on God's responsibility for the sovereign care of the world. It involves taking your life out of God's hands and putting it under your own control. Ultimately, worry is nothing more or less than doubting God. It is an affront to His love and care for us because it is an admission that we are not sure He really loves us.

Thoughts of Criticism

Some people would never criticize anyone directly, but they are filled with criticism in their hearts. Criticism is often a reflection of bitterness within the soul. Every time I see a person criticizing someone else, I wonder what is wrong in that person's own life that is feeding that critical spirit.

I recall hearing a story about a father trying to get some work done while his small son kept insisting that they play together. After a while the father thought, *I've got to find something for my boy to do so I can get back to my work.* He picked up a magazine and thumbed through it until he found a picture of the world. Then he carefully tore out the picture and cut it into several pieces.

I'll make a puzzle out of this to keep him busy, the father thought. Handing the pieces to the boy, he announced, "Here, put this picture of the world back together, and when you are done I'll stop everything and play with you the rest of the day."

The dad thought the boy would never be able to fit all the pieces together. So the little fellow began to work, taking the pieces and taping them together. In just a few minutes he was finished and he took the puzzle back to his father. "How could you be finished already?" the dad asked.

"It was easy," the boy said. "On the back of the world was a picture of a man. When I got the man together right, the world was right, too!"

The reason many people complain that their world is not right is because they are not right. Only when your heart is changed will your criticism subside. A critical, faultfinding spirit will destroy your life and your relationships with others. It will sour everything about you and drive others away.

Thoughts of Torment

Sometimes our minds are bombarded with thoughts of torment. These are disturbing thoughts that seem to come upon us unconsciously. We are tormented by past failures or future worries. The emotional torment of the mind is a terrible thing to experience; it robs us of joy and perpetuates fear and anxiety in every area of life.

I remember talking once to a man who was troubled by deep anxieties, but he could not specifically pinpoint what they were. He lost sleep nearly every night worrying about worrying. This problem is especially difficult for Christians who know they are not supposed to worry. Such a state of mind can actually drive someone to the edge of insanity.

No matter how simple or complex your troubles may seem to be, God has an answer to your problems. He is the God of love and peace, who fills our minds with those positive qualities which can help us overcome wrong thoughts, attitudes, and actions.

Renewing Your Mind

I have found four simple steps about the thought life that are very helpful to me. These steps have enabled me to keep my mind freshly focused on the things of God. I think you, too, will find that they will help keep your mind under the control of the Holy Spirit.

Commit Your Mind to the Son of God

God has a wonderful plan for every aspect of your life. That plan includes the provision of His perfect peace to keep your mind sound and stable. The prophet Isaiah said,

"Thou wilt keep him in perfect peace, whose mind is stayed on thee" (Isaiah 26:3). The mind that is committed to God is "stayed" (resting) upon Him.

If you are struggling with thoughts of temptation or torment, commit your mind afresh to God. Determine to let Him have total control to keep your mind from the bombardment of wrong thoughts. But don't forget you have a part in this, too. You must remain alert yourself to guard your mind from the garbage of ideas that Satan will send your way. If you don't, they can ever so quickly overcome you.

Recently I heard a story on the radio about a 70-year-old man who lived on the streets of Chattanooga, Tennessee. He was discovered by a city worker one day under a pile of trash in the city dump, just before the pile was to be taken to an incinerator for burning. After rescuing him, the worker asked how he got there. The man said, "All I remember is that I went to sleep in a pile of trash and the next thing I knew I woke up in the dump!" Likewise, we cannot afford to sleep for one minute and let evil thoughts dirty our minds.

A clean mind comes in two ways. First, we must clear out all the wrong thinking; and second, we must fill our minds with the truth of God. The same God who saved your soul also saved your mind. You belong to Him now. So, let Him have control.

Just as we need to cleanse our bodies with soap and water on a regular basis, so also do we need to cleanse our minds continuously in the Word of God with a fresh commitment to Jesus Christ. There is nothing more refreshing than a clean, clear mind.

Have you ever noticed how good you feel when you first come out of the shower with your skin so clean that it actually squeaks as you rub your hand across it? Fresh. Pure. Cleansed. In the same way, when our minds have been washed in repentance and committed to thoughts that are pleasing to our Lord, we can know the blessing of having our minds fresh, pure, and squeaky clean.

Feed Your Mind on the Word of God

The psalmist said, "Thy word have I hid in mine heart, that I might not sin against thee" (Psalm 119:11). When we feed on the Word of God, we can expect to grow into spiritual maturity. Life operates on a simple principle: Whatever I feed is going to grow, and whatever I starve is going to die.

If you want to overcome bad thoughts, stop feeding them into your mind. Stay away from that which leads you away from God. Fill your mind with thoughts that will help you to grow in your relationship to God.

Our Lord described His followers as those who "hunger and thirst after righteousness" (Matthew 5:6). The more you learn to hunger for His Word, the more you will be filled with His truth. Only then will you be truly satisfied within your soul.

Fill Your Mind with the Things of God

It's a fact—all of us are going to fill our minds with something. Although many people are accused of being empty-headed, no person is actually without something constantly in his or her mind.

*To think on Christ is to move closer
to becoming like Him.*

The apostle Paul said, "Finally, brethren, whatsoever things are true...honest...just...pure...lovely...of good report; if there be any virtue, and if there be any praise, think on these things" (Philippians 4:8). Notice the imperative command is to think—to focus your attention—on the good things of God. Whatever is virtuous and praiseworthy is worthy of the attention of the believer. When you fill your mind with good things, you will be amazed at the good that will come to your life.

William James, the famous American psychologist, developed what he called the "as if" theory. It merely states that if you think and act "as if" conditions are one way, eventually they will become that way in your life. I don't totally agree with him on this idea, but I do agree that what we fill our minds with is what we have a strong tendency to become. Perhaps that is what the Holy Spirit meant when He moved upon Paul to say, "Let this mind be in you, which was also in Christ Jesus" (Philippians 2:5). To think on Christ is to move closer to becoming like Him.

Focus Your Mind on the Will of God

The ultimate goal of the Christian life is to glorify God by doing His will. That means finding His will according to His Word and doing it with all our heart. The whole purpose of renewing our minds is that we "may prove what is that good, and acceptable, and perfect, will of God" (Romans 12:2).

God has a plan which encompasses every detail of your life. As you seek to live for Him, He will reveal the specifics of that plan to you. The will (Greek, *thelēma)* of God is that which God has decreed for you. The verb "that ye may prove" is an expression of purpose. It means that if you live according to God's purpose you will prove it to be good, acceptable, and perfect.

There are several aspects of God's will for our lives which are clearly stated in Scripture. He wills for us to repent of our sins and receive Christ by faith in our hearts. He wills for us to grow in His Word and to be a witness of His salvation. He wills for us to be involved with other believers through His church. Beyond this, the specific details of His will are normally worked out one step at a time as we serve Him.

It does not matter so much *where* God wants you in His will, but *that* He wants you in His will. Wherever He leads you, what really matters is that you allow Him to lead you one step at a time.

The Bible promises that when we stop worrying and start praying, "the peace of God...shall keep [our] hearts and minds through Christ Jesus" (Philippians 4:7). Being kept (literally, "guarded") by God's peace brings security and stability to our innermost being. So keep your mind filled with God's truth and focused on His direction, and you will find yourself being kept each day in His perfect peace.

9

You Can Handle Your Habits

*A*s I was driving to the office one morning, I tuned into a religious talk show on the radio. On this particular day, a counselor was taking calls from listeners. I'll admit I wasn't paying too much attention, knowing that I would do my own share of counseling that day, until I heard one man's voice. You could tell he was weeping on the other end of the line as he said, "Sir, I'm being destroyed. My life is being absolutely devastated. You see, it's something I've gotten involved with. Up until now, I've been able to hide it from most everyone else, but it's about to cost me everything I've ever wanted or worked for. My problem is, I'm hooked on cocaine. It's got me so bad, I can't live a day or rest a night without thinking about it. At first I thought it was just a habit, but now it's more than that. Now it's my life, and I'm about to lose my mind because of it."

As I heard this poor man, my heart went out to him. I was reminded that he is not alone, for I am convinced that there are countless others who are in the grip of some destructive habit they can't seem to shake. It has become ingrained into their lifestyle, and Satan is using it as a stronghold to wreck their happiness and all that God intended for them to have. I honestly believe it can happen to anyone. And when it does, it can become so much a part of their lives that it sears their consciences and destroys their sensitivity to its wrongness. They convince themselves that they are trapped and there is no way out, so they'll just have to learn to live with it. Of course, that is simply not true.

Destructive habits in people's lives may vary greatly from one person to another. Some are hooked on drugs, while others are addicted to alcohol. Some, like this poor man, are enslaved to cocaine, while others are living in illicit sexual sins. Sometimes these destructive habits involve such socially accepted practices as gossiping, boasting, or just downright pride. No matter what the problem, the end result is still the same. A habitual sin has a hold on your life and seems as if it won't let you go. Instead of your having the habit, the habit has you!

Let Go Before It's Too Late

The book of Hebrews tells us to "lay aside every weight, and the sin which doth so easily beset us" (Hebrews 12:1). In the context of the verse, the writer is using the illustration of one who is running a race. Wanting to make the fastest time possible, the runner lays aside anything which might slow him down in the race. Just as it would be ridiculous for us to run a race carrying a concrete block on our shoulders, it is equally ridiculous for us to attempt to run the race of the Christian life bogged down by a destructive habit.

Whether anyone else knows about that sin is not the real issue. You know about it, and it is destroying you. That means that ultimately, you are the only one who can deal with it effectively. If you want to live a victorious Christian life, you must face the fact that Satan has a grip on your life. If you have been regenerated by the Spirit of God, then God lives within you. Your life is not the domain of Satan any longer. You belong to God and have been indwelt by His Spirit. But even as a believer, you can still struggle against both the flesh and the powers of spiritual wickedness (*see* Ephesians 6:12).

Realize what Satan is doing to you. When you committed your life to Christ, Satan lost his control over you. You were snatched from the gates of hell and delivered into the kingdom of heaven. But now, Satan may be trying to do all that he can to destroy your testimony, negate your faith, and wreck your mind. He will come bringing his temptation, attacking you at your weakest point. Once you give in to that temptation to sin, it will return again and again. As you continue to succumb, that sin becomes a habit in your life. In time, that habit becomes your lifestyle itself. That is when Satan comes along and begins to accuse your soul. "How can you claim to be a born-again Christian and live like this?" he asks. "You are no better than those who are not saved," he suggests. "In fact, perhaps you were never saved in the first place!"

Bondage of Guilt and Doubt

Once you begin thinking like that, you become almost worthless from a spiritual standpoint. A Christian who is filled with doubt and confusion because of a sinful habit in his life will never be able to put forth the spiritual effort and energy to serve God effectively. D.L. Moody once said, "I have never known God to use a discouraged person." That is true, no matter what the cause of discouragement may be. But it is especially true when we are discouraged because we are being defeated by habitual sins.

When you became a Christian, God entered your soul. He adopted you as His child and made you an heir of the kingdom of Jesus Christ. But despite all that God has done for us, He does not eradicate our fleshly nature this side of heaven. That means that you and I still have the potential of committing sin and that sin has the potential of becoming a habit in our lives.

There are two types of habitual sin. The first is unconscious sin, such as gossiping. I belive that most people who struggle with this sin do not deliberately intend to malign others. They do it unconsciously and yet maliciously. When a person struggles with unconscious sin, he or she must be confronted deliberately in order to bring the conscious mind to bear upon the sinful habit.

Second, there are deliberate sins which we consciously commit. These are usually related to fleshly urges within us, like drinking, drugs, or adultery. In order to overcome sins of a physical nature, we must learn to deny the flesh. When someone is trapped in such a sin, that person's body will become accustomed to experiencing that sinful desire. Though a very difficult battle may ensue, we will see later how believers can learn to overcome sins of the flesh.

The ultimate tragedy of habitual sin is that it leaves the participant in bondage. It is as though Satan were wrapping you up like a mummy. The first few loops of sin seem harmless enough, but they are just the first steps. In time, Satan has wrapped up your entire life in bondage to him. You begin to feel trapped and incapable of throwing off that bondage. It is at such a point that many people stop trying to deal with their sin at all. They simply rationalize to themselves that this is the way life is and there is nothing they can do about it. Tragically, they resign themselves to a life of bondage to some damaging habit.

Reasons People Remain in Bondage

As a pastor, I have often questioned why people allow themselves to remain in bondage to sin once they see its awful consequences in their lives. You would think that they would want to do whatever they could to throw it off. But like a great yoke of bondage, that sin seems to have weighted them down. They have so capitulated to it that they have lost all hope of deliverance.

In counseling with people, I have found that there are basically four reasons why they remain in bondage to sin.

Some Lack Understanding

Many Christians simply do not understand that they don't have to put up with such bondage in their lives. They do not seem to realize that Satan does not have an automatic hold on their lives. Now that they belong to God, the potential for victory is within their grasp.

All of the resources of Jesus Christ are available to His children in order to overcome the evil one.

The Bible says, "Whatsoever is born of God overcometh the world: and this is the victory that overcometh the world, even our faith" (1 John 5:4-5). Christ has already won the victory over Satan, sin, and temptation. The Scriptures tell us that in Him we are "more than conquerers" (Romans 8:37). All of the resources of Jesus Christ are available to His children in order to overcome the evil one. When Jesus died on Calvary, He put our sins to death. All of the wrath of God against those sins was poured out at that time. Then when our Lord arose from the dead, He arose triumphant over those sins. The victory has already been won!

Others Don't Realize That Victory Is Possible

You don't have to depend upon a pastor, priest, or rabbi in order to know victory over a habit controlling your life. If you know Christ as your Savior, and He dwells within you, then the potential for victory is already within you. The Bible says, "Greater is he that is in you, than he that is in the world" (1 John 4:4).

When you became a child of God, you became a child of the King. The victory you need has already been settled at Calvary. The Holy Spirit who indwells you can empower you to overcome any temptation that you face in life. You have all the resources within you that are necessary to overcome any sinful habit.

To illustrate this, imagine that you are living in England and you go into a local bank for a loan. You walk in and ask to borrow $1,000. If you are willing to put up enough collateral, they just might loan you the money. But what a difference it would make if Prince Charles himself were to walk into that same bank and ask to borrow $1,000. Because he is royalty, they would instantly make any arrangements necessary to lend him the money. Christian friend, could I remind you that you, too, are a child of the King? You don't have to go through life like a spiritual beggar.

There is no condemnation to them which are in Christ Jesus.

Unfortunately, that is what most of us do. We keep begging God for the things that He has already promised to give us. We tend to approach Him with a timidity that implies, "Lord, You really don't want to do this for me, do You?" By contrast, the Bible assures that God wants to answer our prayers and meet our needs in order to show Himself powerful on our behalf. If you want to overcome some habitual sin, you need to realize that the power of God dwells within your innermost being and that you have within you already all the resources necessary in order to do it.

Some Lack Confidence
in Their Own Spiritual Potential

Whenever sin enters our lives, it draws our attention away from Christ and His indwelling Spirit. This causes a lack of spiritual self-esteem. We get down on ourselves and begin condemning ourselves as viciously as Satan would condemn us. While it is important for us to be convicted of our sin, we must also not allow that conviction to sentence us to a life of self-condemnation. The Bible promises, "There is therefore now no condemnation to them which are in Christ Jesus, who walk not after the flesh, but after the Spirit" (Romans 8:1). Once the Spirit of God takes control of your life and you are able to resist the devil and deny the flesh, you should feel freedom and release because your sin has been paid for by Jesus Christ. However, as long as habitual sin remains in your life, it will rob you of the freedom of spirit which God has intended for you to experience. You will remain downcast in self-condemnation instead of realizing confidence in your own spiritual potential.

Satan delights in causing us to feel inadequate even though we are in Christ Jesus. That is why many people lack spiritual self-confidence. I'm not talking about the kind of self-confidence we drum up on our own. I personally do not place total confidence in Richard Lee. But I can place that kind of confidence in Jesus Christ, who lives within me. I have the assurance of His Spirit, who indwells my heart. Therefore the spiritual confidence that fills our hearts is produced by the Spirit of God Himself.

I believe that many people remain in bondage to sin because they have no real confidence in themselves or in God. They have allowed a habit to take root in their hearts, and they think they can't get rid of it. Tragically, they believe this lie of Satan and are robbed of the delivering power that is literally within them.

A Few Don't Want to Give It Up

I realize this is a strong indictment to make, but I am convinced that there are some who never overcome temptation or break habitual sins because they simply do not want to. They have given in to this sin for so long and enjoy it so much that they will not make the kind of commitment that is necessary to break with it and give it up. They harbor that habit because it feeds the desires of their flesh. Often they will even excuse themselves by saying, "The devil made me do it," when in reality the devil cannot make you sin. He can tempt you and try every trick in the book to get you to stumble and fall, but he cannot make you commit the act itself. That is a decision that you make, and it is an option that you must learn to reject.

How Can I Find Deliverance?

Despite the serious hold habitual sin has on some lives, so much that some actually desire to stay beneath its power, there are those who seek deliverance. Many times I have spent long hours in prayer with people whose hearts were broken over problems with habits that gripped their lives. They come seeking a direction out of their dilemma, and it has been my privilege to share with them principles that help them to be set free.

Take Charge of Your Life

I think the first step that a person must take in successfully handling a habit is to *recognize the need to change.* Most of us will never even try to change unless we feel we have a serious need to. Who likes the bother of changing his or her way of living? Who wants to go through the effort if it's not absolutely necessary? Not many of us. More typically, we all like to live as we have been living until we find there is a serious problem in our lifestyle.

Understand this: Habitual sin is a serious problem! It not only can wreck your family, social, and personal life, but it will also ultimately destroy your relationship with your heavenly Father. God cannot tolerate sin. It is against His nature. Never forget that God is a holy God and that any evil we hold in our lives, sinful habits included, separates us from God. You might be convinced to treat sin lightly, but make no mistake—it is deadly. David said, "If I regard iniquity in my heart, the Lord will not hear me" (Psalm 66:18). The word "regard" (Hebrew, *rā'â*; literally, "see") means "to approve." Simply stated, if we give our approval to our sinful habits, God will not have fellowship with us. Therefore, the need for change is evident.

Confess Your Sins

Second, we should *confess our sinful habits to the Lord.* Confession is, in reality, the recognition of one's sin to another. When we genuinely confess our sins we are agreeing with God that they are wrong. It's not only saying we are sorry for our mistakes, but it is also seeing our sins as God sees them.

Repentance (Greek, *metanoia) is* a change of attitude that leads to a change of action. Genuine repentance results from true conviction of sin—it's when we see sin the way God sees it and we learn to hate it in the way He hates it. When that happens, the habit, which at one time seemed to bring such satisfaction into our lives, is now repugnant to us and holds nothing that we desire.

A number of years ago, during my first pastorate, there was an elderly lady in the church who invited our family to her house for an evening meal. Of course, having just started my ministry there, and knowing that the lady was a longtime member, I made every effort to assure her that we could go. The night came, and after arriving at the house, we sat down for the meal. I could not believe what I saw. Sitting in the middle of the table was a large bowl of collard greens. In case you don't know what collard greens are, they are something like turnip greens, but *so* much stronger in their taste. On each side of the big bowl were plates of biscuits. Suddenly it occurred to me that this *was* the meal. The only meal.

Wanting to be a polite guest, I stomached down the first plate, and our hostess quickly filled it up again. "Oh, Pastor," she said, "I'm glad you like it so much. Here's another plateful." By that time I was just about as green as her collards! After I suffered through the final helping, she kindly sent a plate home with me. You know what was in it, don't you? You guessed it—more collards! I hate to admit it, but somehow on the way home, I accidentally dropped the plate and spilled my prize. They tell me that for six weeks after that, our neighborhood had the sickest dogs in town. I understood exactly how those dogs felt. I was so ill the next day that even now the thought of collard greens makes me sick.

What has that got to do with sin? Well, if we ever understand what sin is, and how sickening it is to God, even the very thought of it will sicken us, too. We will quickly confess and repent of it because we will hate it in the same way God hates it.

Let God Control Your Mind

Next, *make your thoughts captive unto Christ.* One of the most powerful statements in Scripture about overcoming habitual sin is found in 2 Corinthians 10:4-5:

> For the weapons of our warfare are not carnal, but mighty through God to the pulling down of strong holds; casting down imaginations, and every high thing that exalteth itself against the knowledge of God, and bringing into captivity every thought to the obedience of Christ.

These verses clearly state that our war against the flesh begins in the mind. That is why our weapons for conquest are spiritual and not material. The "strong holds" of which this passage speaks are those areas in which Satan has become entrenched in our lives. In describing this conflict, Paul tells us that these strongholds can be cast down only by "bringing into captivity" every thought in obedience to Christ. We are literally to capture our thoughts and focus them upon our obedient servitude to the Lord Jesus.

Can you picture Jesus participating in your habit?

As a young man I was faced with many moral decisions, as we all are. Often my decisions would seem to be in the gray areas of life. Perhaps I desired to do a particular deed or attend a particular function but realized that, although it would violate none of the acceptable values of our society, I still questioned it in my heart. How was I to determine what was right or wrong for me? Well, one day as I was discussing that with my mother, she said to me, "Richard, if you can picture Jesus doing what you are about to do, then do it. If not, then don't!" From that day on, I've tried to live by that guideline.

Can you picture Jesus participating in your habit? If not, you need to bring your mind into captivity to that thought and each time you are tempted, say to yourself, "Would Jesus do this? If not, I won't!" Then each time you deny the habit, God will strengthen you to pull down that stronghold that has its grip on your life.

Resist the Devil

Finally, you must be willing to resist the devil. The Bible urges us, "Submit yourselves therefore to God. Resist the devil, and he will flee from you" (James 4:7). "Resist" is a defensive term. It means that we are to stand against our enemy, the devil. Remember, we are in a war, and we can never hold a neutral stance with our enemy.

Notice also that James 4:7 says that if we resist Satan, he will flee from us. Think of that—we have power over him through Christ! If that is true, which it is, then Satan is not our problem with sinful habits; we are the problem. If you are giving in to those things which are destroying your life, then you must decide the issue. The decision is up to you. If you are willing to do what is necessary, the power of God within you will enable you to overcome your habits. Everything you need for complete and final victory is available through Jesus Christ. Take Him at His word, put His power into action in your life, and you will be set free.

10

Say Goodbye
to Guilt

*S*ome of the most difficult thoughts to control are those that stem from a troubled conscience. Guilt is a form of self-judgment and self-condemnation that we often impose upon ourselves. It produces anxiety, inferiority, fear, and worry. Guilt is a major factor in psychological and emotional problems. If left unresolved, guilt can lead people to commit self-destructive acts such as suicide.

In Psalm 32, we read the words of a brokenhearted man who is struggling with the problem of guilt. In these verses, we read the confession of David as he faced the sin in his own life.

> Blessed is he whose transgression is forgiven, whose sin is covered. Blessed is the man unto whom the LORD imputeth not iniquity, and in whose spirit there is no guile. When I kept silence, my bones waxed old through my roaring all the day long. For day and night thy hand was heavy upon me: my

moisture is turned into the drought of summer (Psalm 32:1-4).

David was one of the greatest men in all of Scripture. But despite a long string of successes, he suffered a tragic defeat that involved a triple transgression. He committed adultery with Bathsheba; arranged for the murder of her husband, Uriah; and lived a lie before the people of Israel. Though initially it seemed that David got away with his sin, he later confessed that the hand of God was against him day and night. Because he was a man of God, he could not sin and get away with it in his own conscience. He was deeply disturbed by the reality of guilt, and it took its toll on him mentally, emotionally, and physically. He felt as though he were losing his strength and that he was about to die.

The guilt that God gives you is intended to draw you closer to Him.

If you have ever felt guilt like that, you can begin to understand the terrible inner pain that David felt. Guilt can take away your sleep, ruin your life, and destroy your relationships with others. Many times I have wondered why a certain individual suddenly seemed to look so terrible. Normally healthy men and women who had no apparent physical problems seemed old and worn before their time. Often, I would discover that they were burdened down with terrible guilt inside and that it was beginning to show in their physical appearance. Guilt can take its toll in many different ways.

If you are struggling with the guilt of some past failure in your life, I want to point you to some principles of truth that I believe can help you. No one on earth can undo the wrong that was done in the past. You cannot go back and relive that moment in your life. The mistake was made, the sin was committed, and the guilt is an automatic consequence of it. But the guilt that God gives you is not intended to destroy you. It is a spiritual and psychological reaction that He uses to draw us unto Himself. Though it is a consequence of our sin, it is not a consequence with which we must live for the rest of our lives. The same Savior who died for our sins also died for our guilt and wants to set us free from it. But if you do not let Him set you free, you will experience depression produced by guilt. Your conscience will become bound by that guilt, and you will find yourself unable to enjoy the blessings of life.

Sources of Guilt

Others: Imposed Guilt

People are experts at putting others on guilt trips. They can actually manipulate others through guilt. Psychologists call this *manipulative guilt*. In other words, people make you feel so guilty that they can get you to do whatever they want. For example, Johnny comes to the dinner table and Mother orders him to eat his spinach. Johnny, like most little boys, hates spinach. He doesn't want to eat it. So mother begins to tell him about the little children who are starving all over the world. While he may think, *What does my eating spinach have to do with starving children all over the world?,* he will assume that Mother must be right, and because he feels guilty, he will eat the spinach. Mother has manipulated him by using guilt.

Teenagers are adept at using manipulative guilt. For example, a teenager will say, "Dad, Billy down the street got a brand-new car from his dad for graduation. I wish I had a dad like that!" That is the same tactic which people use with each other when they say, "If you really loved me, you would do this...." These kinds of guilt-producing tactics are provoked by selfishness on the part of those who use them. And the guilt that results is not genuine guilt, but rather, socially or psychologically imposed guilt.

Satan: Condemning Guilt

The Bible calls Satan "the accuser of our brethren" (Revelation 12:10). Accusation is Satan's greatest tactic to get us to give up on our relationship with God. He accuses us so that we will turn to self-condemnation. In essence, when we make a mistake, he condemns our conscience and implies that we have no hope of ever making it right in our spiritual lives again.

You need to remember that the Bible calls Satan a liar and the father of all lies (John 8:44). Every time that he attempts to condemn you or put you on a guilt trip, you have to determine not to listen to his lies. Now it may well be true that you have made a mistake and are feeling guilty as a result of that mistake. However, the guilt that comes from God is not intended to destroy you, but rather, to draw you closer to Him. Satan uses guilt in a destructive manner by attempting to get us into such a state of self-condemnation that we are of no real value in serving God at all. That kind of guilt is not from God.

God: Gracious Guilt

The guilt that God sends into our lives is an expression of His grace toward us. He cannot sit back and merely allow us to continue in sin until we destroy ourselves. Therefore, He begins to convict us through His Holy Spirit that we should turn away from sin. When we refuse to do so, and persist in our sin, He then allows that guilt to grow. This is the kind of guilt that David experienced. It is as though God were saying, "Listen, I know that you have sinned, and that sin is causing a separation between us. But I want you to repent of it and return to Me." That is what real guilt is all about. True guilt comes from God through our conscience as we are being convicted by the Holy Spirit, who dwells within us. That guilt is designed to drive us back into a right relationship with God.

As strange as it may sound, you can actually become excited about feeling guilty. When you are convicted by the Spirit of God, it is obvious that you are a child of God. When the Holy Spirit within us is so sensitive that He reacts to all sin in our lives by producing the kind of guilt that will cause us to repent, then we can rest assured that God is in control of our lives.

Unfortunately, there are those whose consciences have been seared with sin. They have sinned so many times and suppressed the guilt that results from such sin to the point that their consciences are dulled towards sin. Like it or not, we live in a society full of such people. They have had their consciences seared by a lifetime of deliberate and rebellious sin. Only when they are convicted about the guilt of their sin will they do what is necessary to resolve that guilt and confess that sin to God.

I am convinced that God did not intend for us to carry the burden of guilt for the rest of our lives. All of us have failed in one way or another, and we all stand guilty before God. While our conscience condemns us, the Bible reminds us that God is greater than our hurts and that He will defend us on the merits of the blood of Jesus Christ, which has been shed for us. Thus He gives us the gift of gracious guilt to awaken us to our need for repentance and to turn us back to Him.

Improper Responses to Guilt

How you respond to guilt determines what it can do to you. If you allow yourself to become so overwhelmed by guilt that you are driven to self-despair and even self-destruction, then it is obvious that you have responded improperly. And if you merely sublimate that guilt into the unconscious depths of your mind and thereby sear your conscience, you are also making a choice which is headed toward self-destruction. There are three improper ways to respond to guilt.

Refuse It

Some people just try to block guilt out of their minds. They refuse to feel guilty about anything. They have suppressed their guilt and seared their consciences to the point that they can continue sinning and not ever be deeply convicted about it. This is certainly true of mass-murderers, serial rapists, pathological liars, and others who engage in persistent criminal behavior. Those who refuse to face sin in their lives have the attitude that they have never been guilty because they have never been wrong. They are like the basketball player who charges against his opponent, knocks him down flat, and stands there shocked that the referee has called a foul. Such a reaction shows a refusal to accept guilt. That attitude was manifest in Adam when he blamed his sin on Eve. Cain had that attitude when he refused to take responsibility for murdering his brother Abel.

After Adam and Eve's sin, God had apparently made it clear that they could approach Him with a blood sacrifice. The Bible tells us that Abel was a "keeper of sheep" and that Cain was a "tiller of the ground" (Genesis 4:2). In time, Abel brought a lamb to God for sacrifice, while Cain attempted to bring the fruit of the ground. The Scriptures tell us that God accepted the blood sacrifice of Abel but not the vegetable sacrifice of Cain. A reasonable inference is that this was because the latter represented an offering of self-works.

When God declined Cain's offering, Cain became angry with God and eventually took it out on his brother. Yet even when Cain was angry, God gave him an opportunity to correct the problem. He told Cain, "If thou doest well, shalt thou not be accepted?" (Genesis 4:7). The Hebrew text of this Old Testament passage even implies that the option of an appropriate sin offering was at hand by stating that "sin lieth at the door" and Cain refused to give it.

The audacity of Cain's rebellion is incredible: He refused to acknowledge his own failure, rejected the opportunity to resolve the problem, and turned around and killed his brother out of anger and hostility. It is no wonder that God dealt so severely with Cain when He held him accountable for the murder of his brother. Sadly, even under the pronouncement of his condemnation, Cain asked that the sentence not be too severe, rather than confessing his sin and throwing himself on the mercy of God. He is a perfect picture of a person who has refused to face up to the issue of sin and guilt in his life.

Abuse It

In contrast to those who refuse to face guilt are the people who are so overwrought with guilt that they condemn themselves for everything that ever went wrong in life. They have the "I did it" mentality. They feel that everything that has gone wrong is their fault. I used to have a little puppy like that. One day he tore a bedspread and I had to scold him. From then on, every time I walked into the house he would put his tail between his legs, bend his head down, and crouch on the floor. I guess it was his way of trying to say that he was sorry for tearing the bedspread when he was a puppy. I tried to explain to him that I had forgiven him and that all was forgotten, but he never seemed to get the point. Some people are like that as well— they go through life feeling sorry for themselves and blaming themselves for everything that goes wrong. Unfortunately, they never come to experience the wonderful cleansing and forgiveness which God has made available to them.

This is the mentality of abusive guilt. Many people almost enjoy abusing themselves with guilt because they feel that in some way it will help atone for the wrong that they have done. But there is nothing that you could ever do to pay for the sins in your life. That is why Jesus came—to die for those sins.

Excuse It

There is another category of people who are willing to acknowledge that they have sinned, but then try to excuse their sin as though they are not responsible for it. Several years ago I dealt with a man who had committed an act of cold-blooded murder. As he described to me the details of that murder, he began to ask about the consequences of what he had done. During our talk, I did not sense any remorse or guilt in him at all. So I interrupted him with the question, "How do you handle the guilt that you feel over this murder?"

The man looked at me and said, "Oh, I don't feel guilty. It was God's time for the victim to go anyway. God just used me as an instrument to bring about His will." I asked him to leave my office, fearing he might think *my* time had come.

This man had so rationalized his guilt that he could acknowledge the crime and then excuse the whole thing by blaming it on God. Over the years, I have heard more people use this tactic than any other in trying to avoid the problem of guilt. I have listened to husbands who have blamed all of their problems on their wives and wives who have blamed all of their problems on their husbands. I have listened to young people explain to me that their parents made them run away from home. I have heard people blame things on God, the devil, and the church, but in every one of these cases they never came to grips with their own problems. Excusing your sin and its guilt will never resolve the problem.

Getting Rid of Guilt

Freedom from guilt is not something that we can merely develop within ourselves. It is not something that we can resolve by suppressing it into our subconscious minds or blaming others. Rather, guilt must be acknowledged, the mistake that produced it must be confessed, and our lives must become transformed by the grace of God's forgiveness.

Jesus can undo the errors of our past.

David understood this as he expressed his own inner turmoil in Psalm 32; the turning point came when he finally said, "I acknowledged my sin unto thee, and mine iniquity have I not hid" (Psalm 32:5). He confessed his sin, and it was then that he experienced God's forgiveness. By the end of the psalm, he was able to "be glad in the LORD, and rejoice" (Psalm 32:11). David had experienced the tremendous blessing of God's forgiveness and the cleansing that it brings to the heart of the individual transgressor. He knew what it was to fail, but he also knew what it was to be forgiven.

Understand Your Need

The key to getting rid of guilt is to recognize that only God can take it away and cleanse your conscience. When we realize that we have sinned not only against individuals but against God Himself, then we will begin to understand why it is so important that we have God's forgiveness. I believe that David fully recognized this. He did not try to blame his sin on Bathsheba, or on his circumstances, or on the fact that Nathan the prophet had confronted him. He accepted full responsibility for his sin and confessed it to

God. In so doing, he was able to admit his need and find God's solution.

In his prayer of confession, David said, "Mine iniquity have I not hid.... I will confess my transgressions unto the LORD" (Psalm 32:5). David recognized that his guilt was the conviction of the Spirit of God at work in his soul. He accepted the truth of that conviction and acknowledged his sin to God. As a result, he could say, "Thou forgavest the iniquity of my sin" (verse 5).

Accept God's Forgiveness

It is one thing to understand intellectually that God is willing to forgive your sins, but it is another matter to accept His forgiveness. Many times our consciences so condemn us that we think that by remaining in a state of morbid contrition we are somehow atoning for the sin that we have committed. Unfortunately, such an attitude is contrary to all that the Bible teaches. The Scripture makes it clear that the only atonement for sin is the blood of Jesus Christ. He alone can cleanse and He alone can forgive.

An army chaplain told the story of reaching a young man just before he died on the battlefield in Vietnam. It was evident as he held the boy's hand that he had been mortally wounded and these were the last moments of his life, so the chaplain tried to console him the best he knew how. "Son," he said, "is there anything I can do for you?" "No," the young soldier replied as the memories of his life passed before his eyes. "Sir, what I need now is someone who can *undo* some things for me." That's what Jesus Christ is all about: He can undo the errors of our past. It is our responsibility to accept that forgiveness by faith and to believe that the whole matter has been settled at the cross.

Celebrate Your Victory

One of the most amazing features of David's confession in Psalm 32 is the triumphal manner in which the psalm ends. First, he acknowledged his security in God's forgiveness by saying, "Thou art my hiding place; thou shalt preserve me from trouble; thou shalt compass me about with songs of deliverance" (verse 7). David understood that God was the source of his security and deliverance. Second, he understood that the mercy of the LORD was cause for rejoicing. He announced, "Be glad in the LORD, and rejoice, ye righteous: and shout for joy, all ye that are upright in heart" (verse 11). What a triumphal ending to a psalm of confession and a prayer for forgiveness! David recognized that having repented of his sins, he had every right to rejoice in the freedom of forgiveness.

If you have been struggling with the weight of guilt upon your soul to the point that you can hardly sleep at night or barely make it through the day, rest assured that God's forgiveness is available to you. You may have felt as though your heart would burst or your mind would crack because of guilt. You need not struggle any longer. God's grace is so great and His forgiveness is so full that He offers you complete pardon if you will just accept the cross as sufficient payment for your sins. Like David, you have every right to be glad in the Lord, rejoice, and shout for joy. The New Testament puts it this way: "If we confess our sins, he is faithful and just to forgive us our sins, and to cleanse us from all unrighteousness" (1 John 1:9). When you acknowledge your mistake, confess it to God, and repent of it, your soul is cleansed and the weight and guilt of that sin is gone forever. God's forgiveness is an everlasting forgiveness. When He forgives, He forgets! So why don't you?

Part 4

*Peace in Your
Tensions*

11

What to Do
When You Feel
Like Quitting

I had no sooner settled in behind my desk one Monday morning, planning to get my day started, when my secretary's voice came through the intercom. "Tom and Janet are here, and they are really upset."

"Send them in right away," I answered.

Tom burst through the door in a bolt of anger and frustration, with Janet following behind.

"I've had it with him," she announced abruptly as she sat down. "He's impossible to live with anymore."

"Well, *I'm* the one who has had it," Tom replied angrily. "I just don't want this marriage. I've tried and I'm tired of trying."

"Can we talk about it without exploding?" I asked.

"I'll talk about it," Tom said, "but I still want out."

As we talked together about their problems, it became obvious that they were both burning out on life. Their routines of living had become dull and meaningless. The pressures of their work and their poorly managed finances had them both on edge, and they were taking it out on each other. The kids were getting older and making greater demands on their time, and that wasn't helping the situation either.

After a while, I asked them, "Have you ever heard of electrical overload?" Before they could answer, I went on to explain that is what happens when we plug too many appliances into the same electrical outlet. The circuit overloads and usually throws the breaker or blows a fuse.

"That's what you two are doing," I told them bluntly. "You are so overwhelmed with responsibility and pressure that your emotional circuits are overloaded and you're trying to call time-out on life."

Unfortunately, situations like this happen frequently. Many couples appear highly successful but are under so much stress that they are about to explode. Husband and wife lash out at each other in frustration, and their marriage starts to fall apart—even though in many cases their problems are not being caused by their marriage. Rather, the marriage has become the battleground where they take their frustrations out on each other. But stress overload is not unique to married couples.

The Burnout Syndrome

Burnout is a serious problem throughout our fast-paced, high-stress society. It affects everyone. It seems that every time I turn around I'm reading another book or article on burnout. Businessmen and women are burning out on their jobs. Housewives are burning out at home. Single parents are put under an almost unbearable load. Numbers of teenagers are leaving home, trying to walk away from it all, trying to escape, only to find it much worse on the streets.

Often we see Christians who aren't doing much better than the rest of the world on this account. We who ought to know how to find inner peace and strength often fall victim to the same pressures as everyone else. Jesus said, "Peace I leave with you, my peace I give unto you. . . . Let not your heart be troubled, neither let it be afraid" (John 14:27).

Christ Himself promised to give us peace in the midst of life's pressures. Note that He didn't promise there would be no pressures at all; rather, He promised to give us enduring strength during our times of stress and pressure.

The mature knowledge of this is the key to overcoming burnout. When you feel like quitting, you are focusing on your problems, not God's solutions. When stress has you rattled, your attention is not on God. As believers, we are supposed to be different from the world. We are supposed to know how to live under pressure. People should be able to watch our lives and ask themselves, "How do they remain so cool and calm in these situations?" Their curiosity ought to be attracted to the reality of God's peace in our innermost being.

Christ didn't promise freedom from pressures; He promised enduring strength during our times of stress and pressure.

The real issue comes down to one of pressures or priorities. Your life is going to be dominated by one of these two factors. Every morning when you wake up and start your day, you will be dominated by pressures or priorities. Throughout each day you will be controlled by one or the other.

When we let our lives become driven by pressure, every decision we make reflects that constant badgering within us. And though we may outwardly begin to taste success, the end result will be a bitterness within because our soul will begin to dry up.

Driven people never take time to refresh themselves spiritually. They keep moving hurriedly from one project to another, driven by the desire for conquest and success. When they finally arrive at their goals, they are usually burned out and washed up on life. The wreckage lies all along their pathway to success: a frustrated outlook, neglected loved ones, and a loss of everything that is real in life.

On the other hand, when we properly define our priorities (those factors we consider to come foremost in our personal well-being) and make our decisions accordingly, we can better keep our living in balance. When we put God first in our lives, we are establising a spiritual priority which says that whatever helps us grow in our daily walk with Him is most important. That cannot be neglected on the excuse that we are too busy.

When our priorities include such matters as family togetherness, physical and emotional health, and a positive quality of life, we will learn to say no to distractions which would rob us of the vitality of life. But when our priorities are wrong, we will readily sacrifice all of these for that which has little lasting importance. We end up living to satisfy those unrelenting pressures that can never be satisfied anyway.

Enduring the Pressures

A revealing scripture found in Hebrews 11:24-27 tells us how we may endure the pressures of life. It tells us about Moses, who chose the right priorities for his life. Despite having been raised by the daughter of the Egyptian pharaoh, Moses refused his royal heritage, "choosing rather to suffer affliction with the people of God" (verse 25). The author of Hebrews then tells us that Moses denied the treasures of Egypt and forsook its material wealth and prosperity for the will of God.

From the Old Testament we know that Moses was condemned by pharaoh, and he fled into the wilderness for 40 years. Later, he returned to lead the children of Israel out of bondage into freedom. Along the way, he had many problems and struggles. Pharaoh's army pursued them and they were trapped at the edge of the Red Sea. Moses prayed, and God miraculously delivered them by parting the water. Then in the wilderness of Sin they ran out of food and faced starvation (see Exodus 16:1). Again, God miraculously supplied their need by sending the manna. Every step of the way, even when the people complained, Moses remained fixed on God. He never turned back, despite all the obstacles.

What was Moses' secret? Hebrews 11:27 tells us, "For he endured, as seeing him who is invisible." He endured all the pressures of life by faith in God. He went on with such confidence in God's promises that it was as though he could actually see Him. His faith enabled him to visualize God at work in his life. If we are going to endure the pressures of life, we must do the same.

Identity: Know Who You Are

In spite of being raised in pharaoh's home, Moses knew he was an Israelite. He understood that he had been born into a Hebrew family and that his real mother hid him in a basket during a time of persecution. In desperation she placed the basket in the Nile River and let it go. Eventually, pharaoh's daughter found the baby in the basket. She assumed he was a gift from the gods, since the Egyptians believed the Nile was a god and the source of all life. She accepted the baby as a gift of divine providence, and Moses was raised in pharaoh's court as a member of the royal family. As such, he enjoyed all the privileges of wealth and royalty. He may well have been in line to inherit the throne of Egypt itself.

But one day Moses came to the realization of who he really was. He came to a point of spiritual self-identity. He realized that he was an Israelite and a child of God. He could not deny his identity with his own people, so he turned his back on Egypt. He refused to be called the son of pharaoh's daughter because he wanted to be who he really was.

Today, many people want to be someone they're not. "If only I could be like him," they will often say to me, wishing they were better-looking, happier, or wealthier. This is a problem that affects teenagers and adults alike. They think that if they could be somebody else, they would be happy. But they are wrong. True happiness comes only when you accept yourself for who and what you are in Christ. He alone can transform you into the best person you could ever become by His grace.

A television commercial soliciting recruits for the United States Army says, "Be all that you can be." I want to tell you that you can be all you ought to be and need to be through Jesus Christ. You don't need to be anything other than what He has planned for you to be to His glory.

Your real worth has been determined by God, who gave all He had that you might become His child.

Some of us get down on ourselves to the point that we become so depressed that we are useless. We don't believe we are worth anything, so we act accordingly. I remember my high-school chemistry teacher telling me that the chemical elements of my body were worth only about 95 cents. Thinking about that always discouraged me until I heard a scientist say that each pound of the human body has within it enough atoms to produce 11.4 million kilowatt-hours of electricity. Now, according to the Georgia Power Company, that much energy would cost about $798,000. Think about it: I weigh 170 pounds. That means I'm worth about $135,660,000! It all depends on how you look at it.

In fact, you are worth more than money can buy. The worth of your soul is so great that God's own Son took your sins upon Himself and died in your place on the cross. God cared enough about you that He gave His own Son to die for you. Your worth is not determined by your material prosperity, the house you live in, or the car you drive. Your real worth has been determined by Almighty God, who gave all that He had that you might become His child.

Relationship: Learn Whose You Are

The world can be classified into two groups of people: the saved and the lost. Men classify each other by race, nationality, locality, or socioeconomic status. We tend to view people as black or white, red or yellow, rich or poor, white-collar or blue-collar. But in the eyes of eternity, God sees only two classes of people: those who know Him and those who do not.

The Scripture teaches that there are only two ways into eternity. One is broad and leads to destruction. The other is narrow and leads to eternal life. The Bible also declares that there are two foundations to life: one of solid rock and one of shifting sand. The sand represents the unstable ideologies and philosophies of the world, while the solid rock represents Jesus Christ. Unfortunately, many people have built their lives on materialism and the pursuit of self-gratification, only to find it all blown away like the sand when they come to life's end.

The laws of God are specific and relentless. They always work one way or the other. The law of gravity teaches us why things are held to this earth. Gravity keeps us all from hurtling into outer space. But gravity will also cause you to fall down to the ground if you jump off a tall building. Its force can be positive or destructive, depending upon our choices. Similarly, the law of aerodynamics teaches us how things fly; but when violated, it also tells us why things crash. The laws of physics tell us how things are made, but they can also be used to blow things apart.

Jesus said, "I am the way, the truth, and the life: no man cometh unto the Father, but by me" (John 14:6). That may seem narrow to some, but it is the law of God. If you are going to overcome discouragement, you must know to whom you belong. Moses knew that he belonged with the children of God and acted accordingly. We must do the same. Stop putting yourself down and start acting like a child of the King!

Purpose: Understand Whom You Are Trying to Please

Moses had his hands full once he got the children of Israel across the Red Sea. They complained about everything. They didn't like the food, they ran out of water, they questioned Moses' leadership, and some of them even rebelled. The pressures upon him must have been incredible. But Moses was only interested in pleasing God. Otherwise, he would have cracked under the load.

Can you imagine the people of Israel coming to Moses with their requests? I can imagine that it may have begun with the "Let's Not Leave Egypt" committee. Perhaps they thought Moses had taken things a bit too far and wondered how they would all survive out there in the wilderness. Perhaps next it was the "Red-Sea Crossing" committee. I can just hear them trying to talk him out of using his rod and into trying something more conventional. Next might have come the "Wilderness-Wandering" planning committee. They decided it might be a good idea to stay in the wilderness permanently and build a settlement. Perhaps they envisioned something like Six Flags over Sinai.

We do know from Scripture that Moses faced tremendous resistance from the people at every turn. They were always complaining about something. But Moses never gave in to their complaints; he was determined to please

God. He was not a perfect man; he had his weaknesses, too. He needed Aaron and Hur to hold up his arms, and he appointed 70 elders to help him judge the people's requests. On one occasion, he became angry and smote a rock with his staff, although God had commanded him merely to speak to it. But overall, Moses was a great leader because he kept his focus on God.

You and I can never please everyone. When we try, we only exhaust ourselves in the process. Some people are just impossible to please no matter how hard you try. Someone told me once of a woman who had a grouchy husband who was hard to please. But she loved him dearly and was determined to please him. She got up early one morning, fixed herself up, and asked him what he wanted for breakfast.

"I'll fix whatever you want," she announced.

"All right," he responded, "I'll take freshly brewed coffee, freshly squeezed orange juice, toast, bacon, and two eggs—one fried and one scrambled."

*When you concentrate
on pleasing God, He takes care of
satisfying everyone else.*

Desiring to please him, she set about the task of preparing breakfast. She brewed the coffee, squeezed the orange juice, and fried the bacon. Then she cracked one egg and scrambled it and cracked the other egg and fried it. When everything was ready, she called him to breakfast. He walked in, sat down, and looked at the two eggs. A big frown came over his face. He looked up at her and snarled, "Just as I thought. You fried the wrong egg!"

As incredible as it may seem, that shows how ridiculous some people are. No matter what you do for them, you can't please them. So, you are better off not trying to please them. I had to learn early in my ministry to quit trying to please everybody. People would come to me, saying, "Now don't offend this person because he is related to that person." The requests were endless. Finally, I realized there was only one person I needed to please, and that was God. Once I got that settled in my mind, a spirit of peace came over me.

Often the stress and pressure of life comes from trying to please others. It may be your boss, your husband, your wife, your kids, or your family. But whoever they are, you will never be able to completely satisfy their needs. Only God can do that, and He doesn't want you wearing yourself out trying to do His job. He alone can meet their needs. All you have to do is concentrate on pleasing Him.

The Bible promises, "When a man's ways please the LORD, he maketh even his enemies to be at peace with him" (Proverbs 16:7). When you and I concentrate on pleasing God, He takes care of satisfying everyone else. You don't have to please everyone. Chances are that you can't do so anyhow. Simply trust God with your pressures and determine to please Him with your life.

Direction: Know Where You Are Going

Most people think the Israelites stayed in the wilderness for 40 years because they were lost. Not so! The Scripture tells us that they knew where they were going. Their destiny was the land of Canaan, known to them as the Promised Land because of God's covenant with their forefathers. They remained in the wilderness for 40 years because of rebellion against God's direction for their lives.

But despite all their problems, Moses never lost sight of their ultimate goal. He knew that their final destiny was well worth the wait and the struggle. He kept his eyes focused on the eternal reward of God. You and I must do the same. Whenever it appears that all has failed, that the journey is too difficult, or that the road is too rough, remember where you're going. Pressures seem to ease greatly when our purpose lies clearly before us and we know where we are headed.

My father had a little poem that he would often say to us kids in our times of self-pity and discouragement. I've remembered it through the years—especially when I felt like giving up or thought the winds of good fortune were blowing in everyone else's direction but mine. It goes like this:

> One ship sailed east
> Another sailed west,
> Impelled by the self-same blow.
>
> For it's not the gale
> But the set of the sail,
> That determines where they go!

God will not give up on you as long as you don't give up on yourself. Set your sail and keep on. There will always be rivers to cross and mountains to climb. But God is with you every step of the way. When you falter or stumble, He will hold you up. He will give you direction. He will see you through.

When the great conqueror Napoleon and his armies crossed the Alps, his troops came into battle with the enemy. Napoleon's troops found themselves trapped in a valley, and many began to get killed.

The great leader's heart went out to his men, so he turned to his bugler boy and said, "Son, sound the retreat." The boy did nothing. Again Napoleon said, "Son, blow the retreat or our men will die."

Then the bugler looked at his great general and said, "I'm sorry, sir, but I have forgotten the sound of retreat." Napoleon snapped back, "Then blow whatever you know how to blow!"

The boy placed the bugle to his lips and blew—charge, charge, charge! Napoleon's troops thought, *Help is coming,* and they fought with all their might. The enemy thought, *We must flee because reinforcements must be on their way.* Thus the battle was won and eventually the war—all because one little bugler boy had forgotten the sound of retreat.

Quitting is not an option for the Christian. We have been set free from our old life and we must press on to our new destination. Like the children of Israel, we can't go back to Egypt; it isn't wise to stay in the wilderness; so we must press on to the Promised Land. Like the bugler boy, we must forget the sound of retreat. No matter how long or difficult the journey, it's never right to quit. Keep your focus on the goal and keep pressing on, for victory is straight ahead.

12

Four Thieves That Rob You of Peace

*D*ealing with destructive habits and specific acts of sin is only part of the process of renewing that is to be going on in our minds as we offer ourselves to God. Another aspect of this process focuses on the positive qualities that God wants to develop in our lives. According to His Word, the natural result—the fruit—of His Spirit's work within us is "love, joy, peace, longsuffering, gentleness, goodness, faith, meekness, temperance" (Galatians 5:22-23).

Yet, most of us find our lives at times characterized by one or more of these less-admirable attitudes: worry, fear, anger, and bitterness. We are going to look at each of these in depth, but let me say at the outset that there are not really four problems here, but only one. Worry, fear, anger, and bitterness creep into our lives when we let faith slip away—when we fail to believe that God will keep His promises to us.

Worry

Worry is a terrible way to live, but millions of people are choosing to walk that path every day. Worry is practically an epidemic in our affluent society. Every year Americans spend millions of dollars on tranquilizers in their attempt to conquer worry.

Yet, worry is a choice. Nobody forces you to worry. I doubt your husband or wife woke you up this morning and said, "Honey, please wake up and start worrying." Your boss at work didn't say, "If you want to keep your job, you've got to learn to worry." Neither did the teacher at school say, "Class, for your homework today, go home and worry." It all sounds ridiculous, doesn't it? But it proves the point: Worry is not an attitude someone else forces upon us. It is an attitude that we choose to wallow in ourselves.

I am convinced that God never intended for us to live with anxiety and all the nervous conflict it produces. In the Sermon on the Mount, Jesus told His disciples how to overcome the problem of worry. He said,

> Seek ye first the kingdom of God, and his righteousness; and all these things shall be added unto you. Take therefore no thought for the morrow: for the morrow shall take thought for the things of itself. Sufficient unto the day is the evil thereof (Matthew 6:33-34).

Our Lord understood how to handle the pressures of life. He realized that life was more than meat and drink and the material things of this world. He also understood that the world's goods were not wrong in and of themselves, but that much of the worry that people exerted was in relation to them. It is for that reason that He told His disciples to seek first the kingdom of God, and those things would be added unto them.

Live One Day at a Time

By telling His disciples not to worry about tomorrow, Jesus was trying to help them understand the importance of living for today. None of us have a guarantee of tomorrow;

therefore, we must learn to appreciate what we have today. That is not to say that we cannot plan ahead for the future, for such planning is certainly wise. But what our Lord was trying to help us to see in this passage is that we have no certain knowledge about tomorrow, so we might as well stop worrying about it.

Worrying about the past or future will only destroy the present.

Think about it. Most of our worries are about the future. We focus on the fear of what might happen in the next few days, or next week, or next year. If we are not careful, we can become consumed with worrying about our job, our family, our health, our finances, or whatever. Once you shift your focus from the present to the future, you will fail to do what you ought to do today in order to guarantee a better future. It is today that really counts in your life.

The great thinker Thomas Carlyle said, "Our main business is not to see what lies dimly in the future, but to do what lies clearly at hand."

All the worry in the world is not going to change tomorrow. There is no way that worry is going to assure us a better tomorrow. Worrying about education, marriage, occupation, or even retirement does not make any of those matters come more easily. In fact, most worriers destroy the present by becoming consumed over the past or the future.

Do One Thing at a Time

How often we get our lives into trouble when we scatter our minds in a hundred different directions! The Bible reminds us of this as it talks about a double-minded man being unstable in all of his ways (James 1:8). The apostle Paul had this singularity of purpose in mind when he said, "This one thing I do" (Philippians 3:13). Once he discovered God's plan and purpose for his life, he became totally committed to fulfilling that one goal. Therefore, he said that he would press on to the mark that God had set for him. He became so single-minded in focusing all of his activity toward accomplishing that purpose that he was able to achieve a tremendous amount of service for God in one lifetime.

When all of our activities revolve around the most significant task to which God has called us, everything that we do will contribute to the fulfillment of that purpose. And I believe that God has a unique and specific purpose for the life of every believer. While your life may include many facets of serving the Lord and you may have been gifted with a number of qualities and abilities, there is ultimately one thing God wants you to do. He wants to bring your life into conformity with the image of His Son; He wants to make you so much like Christ that you become a reflection of His glory.

When I was a young student away at school, I roomed with several other guys. We had just about everything you could imagine in our room. And I do mean everything! We thought it was neat to see just how much junk we could put in one dorm room. Every night when we were supposed to be studying, we would close the door and do things like turn on both the radio and the stereo, get out the Monopoly game, and dribble a little basketball. Have you ever tried to study algebra while listening to the stereo and the radio, playing Monopoly, and dribbling a basketball? The grades I sent home at the end of the first quarter taught me a great lesson: You cannot do several activities at the same time and do any of them effectively. You must live life one day at a time and do one task or activity at a time; then God will help you achieve perfect peace of mind.

Trust God All of the Time

In teaching His disciples to overcome the problem of worry, Jesus reminded them that God had clothed the grass which would soon fade away. If He has that much concern about the grass, Jesus asked, "Shall he not much more clothe you?" (Matthew 6:30). He went on to explain that your heavenly Father knows what you have need of and delights to meet those needs. If we are under the care of God, we have nothing to worry about. He can provide us with an inner peace and calm that will enable us to face any of the storms of life. If God can keep the universe going, He can certainly keep us going as well.

When I was a boy, we used to sing a hymn that said,

> Many things about tomorrow
> I don't seem to understand
> But I know who holds tomorrow,
> And I know who holds my hand.*

Those words are a beautiful reminder that Christ is in control of our lives. He not only knows the future, but He also controls the future. Therefore, worrying about the problems of life is a most futile effort. Once I've cast my care upon Him, there is no reason to worry about anything. When you become filled with anxiety you are really saying to the Lord that you do not trust Him to meet your needs. If you are struggling with the problem of worry today, turn your anxieties over to Him by faith. Trust in His love and His goodness to meet your needs. He will not let you down. We who know the Lord have every reason not to worry.

I once heard the story of a man who was carrying a heavy load on his back as he walked down a lonely country road. A farmer drove by in his truck and offered to give him

---

*Ira F. Stanphill, "I Know Who Holds Tomorrow." Copyright © 1950 by Singspiration Music/ASCAP. Renewed 1978. All rights reserved. Used by permission of the Benson Company, Inc., Nashville, TN.

a ride. The man accepted the offer and climbed into the back of the truck. As the farmer drove down the road, he looked into the rearview mirror and saw the man sitting in the back of the truck, with the burden still on his shoulders. Finally the farmer pulled over to the side of the road, rolled down the window, and shouted, "Mister, if I'm carrying you, why are you still carrying that load?"

If God can carry your burdens, then you have no need to carry them yourself.

As foolish as it may sound, that is exactly what we do when we who know that the Lord cares for us continue to fill our minds with care and worry. The Bible tells us that our lives are in the hands of God. But by the way we live, we act like the man who sat in the truck carrying his own burden. If God can carry you through the problems of life, then you need to lay down the burden and trust Him all the way.

Fear

The first step to overcoming fear is to admit that you have it. There is not a single person I have ever known who has not experienced fear in his or her life. It is certainly not a sin to admit, "God, I am afraid." The Bible is filled with examples of men and women who faced fearful circumstances and learned to overcome their fears by the power of God.

Fear is a common emotion. It affects nearly every one of us. In the fourth chapter of Mark, Jesus dealt with the issue of fear. He and His disciples were in a boat and were crossing the Sea of Galilee. As they were crossing the water, a storm suddenly arose and a tempest began to rage. The rain beat upon them and the waves began to lash into the boat. Fearing that they might sink, the disciples panicked and awakened the Lord, who was asleep in the hinder part of the boat. The Bible says,

> They woke him and said to him, "Teacher do you not care if we perish?" And he awoke and rebuked the wind, and said to the sea, "Peace! Be still!" And the wind ceased, and there was a great calm (Mark 4:38-39 RSV).

It is easy to understand their fears. Storms come off the Mediterranean Sea rather quickly and flow inland, sweeping unexpectedly over the Sea of Galilee. The disciples were taken by surprise and caught out in the middle of the lake. Not only can we sympathize, but we can also empathize with their fears. Yet, it was out of this incident that our Lord taught His disciples to overcome their fears.

The Certainty That Fears Will Come

As long as you are living on this planet, you are going to experience storms, difficulties, and troubles in life. There are many people who will try to tell you that Christians never have any problems or troubles. They say that when you receive Jesus Christ as your Savior, your life becomes problem-free from that point on. Unfortunately, that is not true. Most of the people who make such statements either have not walked with the Lord very long themselves, or are simply blind to the realities of life.

Difficulty and trouble are a part of our lives. While some tribulations come as the direct result of our disobedience, as in the case of the prophet Jonah, that is not the only cause of difficulty. There have always been wonderful servants of God who have suffered greatly in this life and done nothing disobedient to bring that suffering upon themselves. In fact, our Lord Himself warned us in John 16:33, "In the world ye shall have tribulation." "Tribulation" (Greek, *thlipsis*) means "affliction." This affliction may be brought on by any one of a number of things. As we mature in our walk with God, we will learn that there are always going to be tough times in life and reasons to feel fearful—no matter how close we are to Him.

Life has variety. Not every day is a sunny day. Some days are filled with sunshine, to be sure, but others are filled with rain. Life itself is not one long mountaintop experience. Some days we are up and other days we are down. I like what one man said about his father, whom he admired very much. His father was a man of great character and dependability. The man wrote a poem about his father and remembered him in this way:

> Whether the weather be good,
>   Or whether the weather be not,
> Whether the weather be cold,
>   Or whether the weather be hot,
> Whatever the weather,
>   He weathered the weather,
> Whether he liked it or not.*

This man was saying that his father had developed the kind of character that was necessary to face the storms of life, no matter what they were or when they came. I realize that this is not a popular concept. There are some people who would prefer to believe that life is one fantastic experience after another. But I must honestly tell you that life isn't that way for most people. While every believer has the right to expect good things from God, we must also recognize that we are still living in a vulnerable body of human flesh. We are subject to disease, difficulty, and death.

---

*From *Pepper 'N Salt* by Vance Havner, copyright © MCMLXVI by Fleming H. Revell Company. Used by permission of Fleming H. Revell Company.

The Solution to Fear Is Faith

In dealing with His disciples, our Lord made it clear that faith and fear cannot mix. As we have more faith, we will have less fear. Somebody once put it like this: Fear knocked at the door of my heart, and when I sent faith to answer the door, no one was there!

In the allegory *Pilgrim's Progress,* John Bunyan told of the soul's pilgrimage through this life. In one scene, two characters, Christian and Hopeful, were tired of traveling down the rough road and chose to journey across By-path Meadow instead. There they were captured by Giant Despair and thrown into Doubting Castle.

For days they were held captive in Doubting Castle. Finally, Christian could stand it no more and cried out, "What a fool am I, thus to lie in a stinking dungeon, when I may as well walk at liberty! I have a key in my bosom, called Promise, that will, I am persuaded, open any lock in Doubting Castle."

Christian reached into his coat and pulled from it the key called Promise. He thrust it into the lock, gave it a turn, and opened the door. Thus Christian and his friend Hopeful were set free to travel again on the King's Highway.

In our humanity it is easy to become imprisoned by fear and despair. But we need not remain there. Trust in the key called Promise and, as you do, your fears will diminish; your despair, no matter how large a giant it seems to be, will flee; and your faith will be set free.

Courage isn't the absence of fear. Courage is acting in the face of fear. There was no question about whether or not Christ loved the disciples. He had proved that to them over and over again. In time, He would prove it in the ultimate degree by giving His life for them on the cross. The real issue at stake was whether or not they had the courage to place their confidence in Him. The question "Carest thou not that we perish?" (Mark 4:38) was an expression of their uncertainty and lack of faith.

What they failed to understand is that it is impossible to have one foot upon faith and the other upon fear. But why were they afraid? Christ had never failed them before. He would not fail them now. And why should we fear? He has never failed us. Perhaps that is the only thing that He cannot do—He cannot fail! It isn't within His possibility. With that in mind, courage should swell within us; and when fear comes, we should hold that fact as a shield against it.

Anger

Anger is one of life's most destructive emotions. It can ruin a friendship, destroy a marriage, or split a home. It can cause you to say and do things that you may regret for the rest of your life. Anger is so powerful that it can erupt like an explosion and leave the irreparable damage of shattered people strewn over the pavement of life. If left unchecked, it will not only destroy your relationships with others, but it will ultimately destroy you.

Let me ask you: Are you a hothead? Do you have trouble with anger? Are you the kind of person who gets mad at the drop of a hat and will even be glad to furnish the hat?

Or perhaps you are one of those who always seem to remain cool on the outside while hot on the inside with anger. Some people are experts in hiding their anger like that. They try to give the impression that nothing bothers them. They appear to have their act together. Others might blow up, but not these people. They don't let anybody see their temper. They keep their anger all inside for a while; but because they never admit it and come to terms with it, their anger eats them alive from the inside out.

The Causes of Anger

Let's begin by looking at the three basic causes of anger. Each of these causes feeds the problem of anger in our lives. Left out of control and unchecked by the power of the Holy Spirit, they can ultimately destroy us.

Fear

Many times we get angry because of fear. Something happens that frightens us. All of a sudden we are fearful, but after we calm down, we become angry. Have you ever had a close call that frightened you? Perhaps you were driving down the highway minding your own business when someone pulled out in front of you and ran you off the road. You slammed on the brakes and skidded to a stop. At first you were frightened out of your skin. Then you calmed down, got hold of yourself, and blew up!

Your initial reaction was to thank God that you were not seriously hurt. But then you got red in the face, started thinking about what happened, and yelled something like, "Where did that guy get his driver's license?" You were afraid, and then your fear turned to anger.

Perhaps you have gone to bed at night hoping for a peaceful night's sleep. Suddenly, at 2:00 A.M., your telephone rings, shattering your sleep. Startled, you leap out of bed and start running to the phone. As you race through the dark you just know something terrible must have happened. Is it my family? Who died? Who in the world would be calling me at this hour? You grab the phone and pick it up just in time to hear someone hang up on the other end! You become so upset with the caller that you can't go back to sleep. There goes another night, and your fear turns into anger.

Frustration

Another cause of anger is frustration. It may not be as stunning as fear, but it feeds anger nevertheless. Have you ever been frustrated because you couldn't pay your bills? Or, perhaps you tried to clean the house in preparation for company and became frustrated because the kids kept messing it up. Dads get frustrated at work, moms at home, and teenagers at school. Frustration is a part of life. When we don't handle it right, it can lead to anger.

Perhaps you have studied long hours for a school exam, only to fail it. The normal human tendency is to become frustrated and want to blow up at the teacher. You may have taken piano lessons and practiced diligently, only to perform miserably. Your frustration turns to anger and you would like to break the piano in half!

Remember the frustrations Moses faced as he tried to lead the children of Israel? The Bible tells us that Moses was the meekest man who ever lived. He led the children of Israel out of Egypt in the great exodus to the Promised Land. He led them across the Red Sea on dry ground and then through the wilderness of Sinai. Despite all of his patience, he finally lost his cool in the wilderness of Zin. We read about it in Numbers chapter 20.

There we see that even though the people of Israel had seen God miraculously provide for their needs time and time again, they began to blame Moses because they had run out of water. It's an old tactic: When all else fails, blame the preacher!

The people began to chide him (Numbers 20:3) which means they yelled and screamed at him. Moses tried to remain calm through it all. He went to the Lord to ask Him what he should do. God told him to take his rod, gather the people together, and *speak* unto the rock and "it shall give forth his water" (verse 8). But in his frustration Moses became angry and *smote* the rock twice instead (verse 11). Moses had endured all he could take. He had put up with enough of their bickering, complaining, and screaming. In essence, he was saying, "If you want water, get it yourself."

As Moses hit the rock, water gushed out for all the people to drink. But he had openly disobeyed God by striking the rock, and because of that one act of anger, provoked by frustration, Moses was denied entrance into the Promised Land.

Frustration means to be provoked out of control. When Moses was provoked out of control, he lost his temper and with it he lost some of his leadership. The tragedy with anger is that it can do irreparable damage.

Hurt

Another cause of anger is hurt. Sometimes we blow up because we have been deeply hurt by something someone said or by some thoughtless thing someone did. People may not even intend to hurt us, but they do.

Perhaps someone has let you down. Your disappointment turns into hurt, and then anger. It can be almost anything: a broken promise, an unfaithful partner, a forgotten anniversary. Whatever may have happened, you hurt for a while. You cried all you could cry. You grieved all you could grieve. Then you thought, *How could they do this to me? To me … of all people! I love them. Just look at all I did for them.* Then you internalized the hurt, and the hurt became anger, and anger turned into revenge. You began thinking, *I'm going to get even. I'm going to show them how much they hurt me. They are going to get what is coming to them.* Before you knew it, your emotions were out of control.

That kind of thinking, I'm sorry to say, is not unusual. It is a problem almost all of us have to deal with from time to time. It's a part of our makeup as individuals. Everyone has the psychological capacity for anger. The biblical term for "anger" means "any natural impulse." In the original Greek text of the New Testament it conveys the idea of *energy.* Anger is a form of human energy that may be used for good or evil. Anger may make one person become a murderer and cause another person to defend himself against a murderer. Whichever response we choose, anger, like any other form of energy, must be released.

The Cure for Anger

What can we do about anger? Since it is an emotional response that can become a sinful action, it is important that we learn how to cure it. Anger is a problem that is common to all of us, although it affects some people more than others. At the same time, we dare not excuse it or simply hope that it will go away. We must discipline our-selves to deal with it.

Reverse It

The same passage of Scripture that warns us against the problems of anger tells us what to do about it. Ephesians 4:32 states, "Be ye kind one to another, tenderhearted, forgiving one another, even as God for Christ's sake hath forgiven you."

The person who has a problem with anger has a deeper problem with unforgiveness. It's that unforgiving spirit that keeps feeding anger. It calls out for revenge. It is that attitude which says, "I'm not going to forgive you because you deserve my anger."

Do you remember what Jesus said as He hung on the cross? "Father, forgive them; for they know not what they do" (Luke 23:34). You need to let God forgive you before you can forgive anyone else. Anger cries out, "I'll never forgive you." But the cross of Christ cries out, "Father, forgive them."

It is only in the cross that we can find true reconcilia-tion with God and man. We who have been forgiven must learn how to forgive. The real problem with anger is not our temper; it is our unforgiving spirit.

Redirect It

In order to fully correct the problem of anger we must learn to take positive steps to redirect our relationships. First, you need to ask God to forgive you for the sin of anger. Second, you need to ask those you have offended to forgive you for your anger. Third, you need to forgive yourself.

Once you have taken these steps, you will be able to concentrate on rebuilding your relationships with others. You will never grow to maturity in your Christian life until you learn how to deal with anger. Only then will you be able to respond with kindness, tenderheartedness, and forgiveness in every situation in life.

The writer of Proverbs put it this way: "He that is slow to anger is better than the mighty; and he that ruleth his spirit than he that taketh a city" (Proverbs 16:32).

The opposite of anger is love. It is often the missing ingredient in our lives. A popular song once said, "What the world needs now is love." Not only does the world need love, but so do a lot of Christians. Love is the essential dynamic that makes life worth living. It is the ultimate expression of our concern for one another. Those who know how to love can overcome the problem of anger.

The process works like this: Anger is the problem; forgiveness is the cure; and love is the result. Once we learn how to forgive those who hurt and wrong us, we can learn how to love them. Usually, we are hurt the most by the people we love the most. It is a tragedy when people spend the rest of their lives hating the person they really love.

Are you angry with someone? Why don't you settle it right now? Don't let the sun go down on your wrath. Deal with it today. The sooner you do, the happier you will be. God loved you so much that He forgave your sins. The least you could do is to forgive those who have sinned against you.

Bitterness

Bitterness is a destructive power which can drain your life of joy. In Luke 15 we see the problem of bitterness in the life of the older brother in the story of the prodigal son. When the prodigal son returned to his father's house, he was received in forgiveness and restored to his rightful position of sonship. The father ordered that the best robe be placed upon his shoulders, that a ring be put on his hand and shoes on his feet, and that a banquet be held in his honor. He announced to one and all, "This my son was dead, and is alive again; he was lost, and is found" (Luke 15:24).

The whole story of the father's restoration of the prodigal son is one of the most beautiful in all of Scripture. It certainly expresses the love of God for the sinner as well as the fallen saint. He is a Father of mercy who delights to call His children back to Himself.

But there is another side to this account that is often forgotten. It is the story of the elder brother. The Bible tells us that as the family began to celebrate the prodigal's return, the elder brother was at work in the field. Hearing the noise of the celebration, he came to the house and discovered that his brother had returned home. He was in shock. He could not believe what was happening. After all, he was the one who had been there all this time with his father. He was the one who remained faithful when his younger brother had deserted them. And now his despicable brother, who had caused much grief, had returned home, and his father was hosting a party. The Bible says that "he was angry, and would not go in" (Luke 15:28).

Is God Really Fair?

When we think about it, it does seem rather unfair. Here this elder son had been faithful to work in the fields day after day, sweating to help earn the income, while his younger brother had been away in a far country wasting his inheritance on harlots and wild living. But look who the party was for! The elder son's heart began to boil with bitterness toward his younger brother.

The father saw what was happening and came out to the elder brother and questioned his attitude. The conversation must have gone something like this:

"Father, what do you mean, asking me why I'm upset? Don't you remember when my brother left, I was the one who stayed faithful? And now look at what it's gotten me!"

"But, son, don't you understand? Your brother was lost, and now he is found. We thought he was dead, but now he has come home—he's alive," said the father.

"I don't care," said the elder brother. "I'll bet if I had blown the family income like my spoiled little brother did, you and everybody else would have just written me off."

His anger was not merely a reflection of sibling rivalry. Rather, it was a reflection of everything that was wrong in his life. He had become bitter toward his brother, and that bitter spirit had warped and twisted his own understanding until he was more concerned about his own feelings than the fact that his repentant brother's life had been saved.

The elder brother's attitude is typical of those who live their lives centered on self more than on others. Our Lord used this story to speak to the people of Israel about their attitudes toward those who had wandered from the commandments of God. The self-centered attitude that asks, "What's in it for me?" is also quite prevalent in the lives of Christians today. Sometimes it seems to ooze out all over. So it was with the elder brother; this attitude can be clearly detected in his response to the situation.

The Results of Bitterness

When bitterness is allowed to remain, it will result in the destruction of those elements of life that are essential for maintaining our balance and joy.

It Destroys Your Perspective

Bitterness clouds our spiritual vision. It causes us to become blinded to the reality of life itself. Once you become bitter and proud, your entire spiritual perspective is blurred. That's the way it always is with pride. It causes people to think more highly of themselves than they ought.

I remember reading about the American humorist Will Rogers. As the story goes, one day a young woman came to him and said she was worried about having too much pride. "Why?" he asked. She said, "Well, every morning when I look into the mirror I think about how beautiful I am." Will Rogers looked at her and said, "I'm sorry to tell you this, young lady, but that's not pride, that's a mistake!" Bitterness and pride will always lead to a wrong perspective of self and others.

When the father responded to the elder brother, he said, "Son, thou art ever with me, and all that I have is thine"

(Luke 15:31). He was reminding his elder son that the celebration for his brother's return had cost him nothing. The father was also reminding the elder son that he had not forgotten the son's faithfulness and devotion to him. He was trying to help his son see that the extension of forgiveness to the younger brother was not intended in any way at all to be a rejection of the older one. The father had the right perspective on the situation, but the elder brother did not. His perspective was clouded by bitterness.

It Destroys Your Usefulness

As long as you have a bitter spirit, you are useless in serving God. There is almost no way that you can be involved in a positive ministry to others because of the bitter attitude within your own soul. Once you allow yourself to get in that condition, you will drive people away from you more than you will be able to point them to the Savior.

Let me remind you that there is nothing more important than being used by God. There is nothing more wonderful or fulfilling than to know that God is working through your life to touch the lives of others. In contrast, there is nothing that will destroy your spirit any more than to know you are no longer being used of God. Remember that you were born into the family of God for a specific purpose. That is why you were created, and that is why you were born again. But when you become bitter, your usefulness greatly diminishes.

I often think of King Saul in the Old Testament as an example of one who developed a bitter spirit. The Bible tells us that Saul was tall and handsome and a man whom the people selected to be their leader. But something tragic happened in Saul's life. We read that he was envious of David because of David's success against the Philistines, and in particular, against Goliath. As a result, Saul became angry and embittered toward David. In his state of bitterness, he began to isolate himself from his advisors. He developed a critical spirit and even turned against his own son Jonathan. On more than one occasion he actually attempted to kill David.

The real tragedy is that David was the one person who could have delivered Saul from the Philistines, but Saul drove David into the wilderness, where the latter became a fugitive. In the meantime, the Philistines mounted a major assault against Saul. In the battle, Jonathan was killed and Saul severely wounded. Saul then took his own life. The sad truth is that Saul died more from his own bitterness than he did from his defeat in battle.

The Remedy for Bitterness

There is no problem which comes into our lives for which God does not have a solution. As we examine the story of the prodigal son and the father's dealing with the elder brother, we find the solution to the problem of bitterness.

He Reminded Him of Who He Was

When the father said to the elder brother, "Son, thou art ever with me," he was reminding the son of his position within the family. It does not matter how bitterly you may have turned your heart from God; if you are a true believer, God is still living within you, He has promised that He will never leave or forsake you, and He will keep that promise. You are His child, and through His grace and keeping power you forever will be. When you remember who you are and that you really belong to the Father, you will realize that there is no excuse for being bitter.

He Reminded Him of What He Had

The father reminded the elder brother, "All that I have is thine." While the prodigal son had been restored with a banquet of celebration, the fact remained that he had blown his inheritance. The father had to remind the elder brother that his inheritance was still due him. As I read this, I am reminded that all too often we forget the inheritance that we have in Christ. We start feeling sorry for ourselves because of some little insignificant problem that has

*All that God has given to Christ,
He has also made available
to you.*

occurred in our lives, and we get our attention off the fact that we are His heirs. There is no reason to go around feeling sorry for yourself. All that God has given to Christ, He has also made available to you as His joint heir. As children of God, we have far more than the rich and famous.

He Reminded Him of What He Needed to Be Doing

The father reminded the elder son that his brother had been lost and was now found. He further reminded him that there was appropriate need for rejoicing and reconciliation. In essence, the father was explaining to his son that his bitterness was destroying his relationship with him as well as with his brother. The appeal of the father was the appeal of mercy versus self-righteousness. It was the request of grace versus judgment.

It has always caught my attention that there is no conclusion to this story in Scripture. The father explains why they ought to be rejoicing and the scene finishes without ever telling us the ultimate response of the older brother. I am convinced that our Lord told this story to urge the self-righteous people of His own day to open their hearts and lives to genuine forgiveness of others. He wanted to help them break through the barriers of bitterness and discover the grace of forgiveness. But He left the decision up to them.

In the same manner, when God deals with our lives today, He leaves the final decision to us. If you have become bitter toward someone else and that bitterness has warped your personality and damaged your relationships with others, it is up to you to decide to do something about it. You can overcome the curse of a bitter spirit. But you can do so only when you allow the love of God to fill your heart and soul with an attitude of understanding which leads to reconciliation and restoration.

13

Finding
Perfect Peace

*T*he world knows little about genuine peace and contentment. Its values are usually based upon social success and material prosperity. The deep, settled peace of mind and soul often eludes the average American. Most of us are disturbed by problems in our country or the instability of world affairs. Our own president has said, "We live on the verge of Armageddon." Last year alone, according to the U.S. Department of Vital Statistics, 31,482 Americans decided they had had enough and took their own lives.

Yet, our Lord Jesus promised us a peace that surpasses human comprehension. He said, "Peace I leave with you, my peace I give unto you: not as the world giveth, give I unto you. Let not your heart be troubled, neither let it be afraid" (John 14:27). He has promised us peace of heart and mind. This is a peace that is rooted deep within the soul of those who know Him as their Lord and Master.

I would like to share with you some principles for peace that I have found helpful in my own life. I believe that you too can know this deep and abiding peace that comes from God. It is the automatic result of His Spirit living within you.

Come to Terms with Your Past

Many people are haunted by something in their past that prevents them from having peace in the present. Some will say, "Just forget it and go on." But it's not that easy. Most of us get bogged down by guilt and can't seem to shake it. When we try to suppress our feelings, we only rob ourselves of true joy and peace. The stress of guilt robs us of peace and leaves us with the heartache of unconfessed sin.

Until you come to terms with sin in your life, you will never conquer it. By this I mean that you must admit (confess) your sin and turn away from it (repent). Only then can you really forget it because it is under the blood of Christ.

Remember, David tried to hide his sin and it didn't work. He had committed the multiple sin of adultery and murder. He had taken Bathsheba and then had her husband Uriah killed. In his mind he rationalized that he had made a mistake, but he would simply marry Bathsheba and go on with his life. However, the Scripture reveals that he was grieved in his heart because guilt was tearing at his soul.

The Living Bible describes his plight like this:

> There was a time when I wouldn't admit what a sinner I was. But my dishonesty made me miserable and filled my days with frustration. All day and all night your hand was heavy on me. My strength evaporated like water on a sunny day until I finally admitted all my sins to you and stopped trying to hide them. I said to myself, "I will confess them to the Lord." And you forgave me! All my guilt is gone (Psalm 32:3-5).

What a marvelous affirmation this is of the power of forgiveness and the peace that it brings. The key to finding inner peace is to confess your sins and lay them at the foot of the cross. Trying to forget them will not remove them from your memory. Only God can erase them from your heart and set you free.

Perhaps you have made a serious mistake recently. Perhaps it was an error in judgment or a character weakness that has flawed your life. You have tried to forget it, but its memory still haunts your soul. It may be a particular day you would like to forget. Perhaps it was a night of sin that you wish had never occurred.

*God offers more
than temporary relief; He offers
everlasting forgiveness
and peace.*

I'll just put it behind me, you have tried to tell yourself. But somehow it won't go away. Let me remind you again that you can't rid yourself of guilt alone. You must turn it over to God by confession and submission to Him. Only then will you find true and lasting peace. He offers you more than temporary relief; He offers you everlasting forgiveness and peace.

Forgiveness comes in two stages. They are distinct, but inseparable, acts. First, *we must seek forgiveness from God,* and second, *we must forgive ourselves.*

Dr. Charles Allen tells an amusing story he read in a newspaper in Wichita, Kansas. It was about a man who tried to forgive himself for a speeding ticket. A terrible snowstorm hit the city on the day he was scheduled to go to court. When he arrived, the court was closed because of the inclement weather. He waited for the judge and the accusing officer, but they never showed up. So the man finally penned a letter to the judge and left it on the door. It went like this:

I was scheduled to be in court on February 23 at 12:15 P.M. It was concerning a traffic ticket. Well, when I arrived, I was surprised to find I was the only one there. No one called to tell me the court would be closed, so I decided I would go ahead with the hearing as scheduled, which meant that I would have to be the officer in charge, the accused, and the judge. Now, as officer in charge, I had given the accused a ticket for going 45 in a 35 MPH zone. But I had to admit I was only estimating his speed. As the accused, I admitted I was going more than the speed limit of 35, but just a few miles per hour faster. As the judge, I was angered that this accusing officer would only estimate the speed, so being the understanding man that I am, I decided to throw the case out of court. But I better not let it happen again.*

Although I'm sure this judge didn't forgive the offense so easily, at least it is evident that the man had forgiven himself. But our eternal God, the judge of all humankind, is willing and wanting to forgive us if we ask Him. And once forgiveness is sought with repentance, then and only then can we honestly, fully, and finally come to terms with our past.

Remember, when God forgives, He forgets. Someone told of a man who came to God about a sin that had long been repented of. He said, "God, I want to talk to You about this particular sin." God replied, "What sin?" God had forgotten. You don't need to be hindered by your past. You don't have a sinful past. It has all been washed away by the blood of Jesus Christ.

---

*Charles L. Allen, *Victory in the Valleys of Life* (Old Tappan, NJ: Fleming H. Revell Co., 1984).

Accept God's Plan for Your Life

We hear a lot today about prosperity. Most Americans live for the almighty dollar. Ours is a society that is intoxicated with material prosperity.

If I could only get that mink coat or diamond bracelet, many women think, *then I'd be happy.*

If I could just afford a new Mercedes or a Jaguar, the men think, *then I'd really be somebody.*

Many of our families are pushing themselves to work more and more in order to get ahead financially. But in their pursuit of prosperity, they often drive themselves to personal and emotional collapse. In other words, the means (overwork) destroys the goal (financial success).

True prosperity is the peace and contentment God gives to us in the face of adversity.

Not only are we consumed with consuming, but some have even tried to get God to help them in this obsession. Prosperity theology has become very popular today. Some people call it "name it and claim it." Others call it "blab it and grab it." Either way, the concept says that God has promised to bless us if we trust Him by faith. Based upon this, they distort the idea of God's blessings to mean that if you take God at His Word, you can get all you want from Him by holding Him ransom to His own promises. It is really a theology of greed that is built upon the faulty premise that we deserve material blessings from God.

God's value system is quite different from that of the world. His view of prosperity is essentially spiritual, not material. His view is expressed in 1 Timothy 6:6: "Godliness with contentment is great gain." God's view of prosperity ("great gain") is based upon two spiritual qualities: 1) godliness and 2) contentment. Godliness is the quality of spiritual piety that enables us to be like God in the character of our lives. Contentment is the quality of satisfaction and sufficiency. In this context, it is derived from God Himself. Thus, the truly successful person is the one who has found contentment in a godly life. Being able to put your head on a pillow at night and know that your soul is clean is the real key to peace with God and yourself.

Godliness is not a characteristic we can attain or produce by ourselves. It is that Godlike quality which results from a heart that is clean before God. It comes as a result of confession and repentance. Contentment is the inner, abiding peace of God regardless of outward circumstances.

The apostle Paul understood this kind of inner peace. Despite being beaten, imprisoned, rejected, shipwrecked, and even left for dead, he knew the true source of peace. He said, "I have learned, in whatsoever state I am, therewith to be content" (Philippians 4:11). It was in this context of talking about his sufferings and difficulties that Paul wrote, "I can do all things through Christ which strengtheneth me" (Philippians 4:13).

If you want to talk about true prosperity, this is it! True prosperity is the peace and contentment God gives to us in the face of adversity. Knowing that your sins are forgiven and that you can have inner peace and strength for today is the greatest success anyone could ever know. This peace is greater than wealth or riches. It is the most valuable quality we could ever possess.

On Monday, October 19, 1987 (a day that has since been labeled "Black Monday"), the stock market took a terrible plunge and nearly collapsed. It was the worst day for many investors in recent history. The results were catastrophic. People took their own lives in violent acts of suicide. One man walked into his stockbroker's office and shot and killed his broker. Then he turned the gun around and killed himself. Why? All because of money. That poor, confused man thought that money was the key to prosperity. And in that tragic moment, he lost what life is really all about.

Money and material possessions can never buy you peace of mind. That kind of peace only comes from God working in your soul. Only when He is in control of your life will you experience the great prosperity of godliness and contentment.

Concentrate on the Present

You cannot go back and relive the past. It is over and gone. Nor can you live tomorrow until it comes. Too many people are so caught between the failures of yesterday and the fears of tomorrow that they cannot enjoy today. But today is your only guarantee. Learn to live it to the fulfillment of God's will. The psalmist said, "This is the day which the LORD hath made; we will rejoice and be glad in it" (Psalm 118:24). He was talking about learning to find our joy in the blessings of today.

Our Lord said, "Don't be anxious about tomorrow. God will take care of your tomorrow too. Live one day at a time" (Matthew 6:34 TLB). When we become overwhelmed by the pressures of life, we get bogged down by the failures of the past or worried about the fears of the future. Either way, we lose the joy of today.

Worry has been defined as "building bridges over rivers you will never cross." True peace comes when we stop worrying and start trusting God to meet our needs. The country singer was right when she sang, "One day at a time, sweet Jesus, that's all I'm asking from you. Lord, help me today, show me the way, one day at a time."*

---

*One Day at a Time," written by Marijohn Wilkin and Kris Kristofferson. Copyright © 1973, 1975 by BUCKHORN MUSIC PUBLISHERS, INC. (BMI) International copyright secured. All rights reserved. Used by permission.

Discover Life's Purpose

God has saved you for a purpose. Find out what it is and give yourself wholly to it. Life is not a meaningless journey. It is an opportunity to discover God's will and purpose for your life. People often feel that their life is a merry-go-round that keeps going in circles but never goes anywhere. They get up in the morning, go to work, come home, eat dinner, watch television, and go to bed—only to get up the next day and do it all over again.

*God has a purpose
for you that no one else
can ever fulfill.*

While that may be a necessary part of a daily routine, it is not the ultimate purpose of your existence. God created you as a unique individual to fulfill a specific purpose in life. When He redeemed you by faith in Christ, He established a purpose for you that no one else can ever fulfill.

The Bible is filled with examples of people who discovered God's purpose for their lives. Abraham was a nomadic herdsman who became the father of the Hebrew nation. Joseph was a slave in Egypt who became the grand vizier, second only to pharaoh. Gideon was a cowardly thresher of wheat who became a mighty warrior who delivered Israel. Ruth was a Moabitess whose devotion to her mother-in-law resulted in her becoming an ancestor of the Messiah. Esther was a Jewish orphan who became queen of Persia and saved the Jews in that empire from destruction. Mary was a young virgin in Nazareth of Galilee who gave birth to

God's Son. Peter was a simple fisherman who caught a vision of what God wanted to do with his life and became one of the apostles. Paul was a legalistic Pharisee who discovered Christ on the road to Damascus and became the greatest missionary evangelist of all time.

Each of these individuals discovered God's divine purpose for his or her life. Each learned that God is no respecter of persons. He will use all those who willingly surrender their lives to Him. The same is true for you and me. There was a time when I simply and routinely went about my daily duties. I was faithful, but my life had no zeal or zest. I had no ultimate purpose to what I was doing. I wasn't even very excited about life. But one day God clearly revealed His cause and purpose for me.

When I learned why I was here, I began to get excited about life. I made His cause my cause, and I made His purpose my purpose. I learned that God had a specific plan for my life. I began to realize that I was called of God to serve Him and that no one else could fulfill that service like I could. Once you come to grips with that truth, you will never be the same again—never! Helen Steiner Rice said it like this:

> Life without purpose
> is barren indeed—
> There can't be a harvest
> unless you plant seed,
> There can't be attainment
> unless there's a goal,
> And man's but a robot
> unless there's a soul...
> If we send no ships out,
> no ships will come in,
> And unless there's a contest,
> nobody can win...
> For games can't be won
> unless they are played,

And prayers can't be answered
   unless they are prayed...
So whatever is wrong
   with your life today,
You'll find a solution
   if you kneel down and pray
Not just for pleasure,
   enjoyment and health,
Not just for honors
   and prestige and wealth...
But pray for a purpose
   to make life worth living,
And pray for the joy
   of unselfish giving,
For great is your gladness
   and rich your reward
When you make your life's purpose
   the choice of the Lord.*

Depend upon God's Promises

The Bible is filled with the promises of God. We need to claim each one by faith and activate its truth in our lives. Some folks like to say, "If God said it, I believe it, and that settles it!" The fact of the matter is, if God said it, that settles it, whether we believe it or not.

Sometimes we ask, "How can I be sure God really said this?" or, "How can I be sure this is what it means?" I realize we must interpret each promise in its proper context. But I also believe that we need to take those promises which apply to us and activate them by faith.

---

*From *Gifts from the Heart* by Helen Steiner Rice (p. 51). Copyright © 1981. Published by Fleming H. Revell Company. Used by permission of the Helen Steiner Rice Foundation.

In Hebrews 4:3, we read an amazing truth. It says there that God's works "were finished from the foundation of the world." In other words, God had already provided the answer to your every need before the world was ever formed. With His divine foreknowledge He looked down the corridor of time, saw your future problem, and provided just exactly what you would need. Since the beginning of the world, God has had in His storehouse of blessings the perfect provision for your problem.

"But you don't know how big my problem is" you may object. Perhaps *I* don't fully understand. But *God* does, and He is greater than all your problems combined. You object because you have your attention focused on your problems instead of on God. Once you comprehend the greatness and magnitude of God, you will see how tiny that problem really is.

Remember that He who lives within you is greater than all of your problems.

We live on a planet that is part of a solar system that is part of a galaxy called the Milky Way. Scientists tell us that if we could travel at the speed of light (186,281 miles per second), it would take us over 100,000 years to travel from one end of the Milky Way to the other! And those same scientists tell us that there are millions of galaxies like the Milky Way in our universe. That is almost beyond what the human mind can comprehend.

But as big as our universe is, it is not as big as God. He is the one who spoke it all into existence. He is the one whose majesty and greatness go beyond the stars. And, yet, He is the one who knows your name, who numbers the hairs of your head, and who loves you and cares about your problems.

Do you really think you have a problem that He cannot handle? When all the personal, emotional, financial, and spiritual problems of life come upon you, remember that He who lives within you is greater than all of them.

How can we find peace in a troubled world? We can find it in a personal relationship with the God who made this world. Even when the world threatens to blow itself apart, we can rest assured that God is in control. That means He is in control of the details of your life as well. You need not spend fruitless hours worrying about life. You have the gift of eternal life within your soul. Your life is co-eternal with the life of God. You shall live forever in His care and keeping.

Pause for a moment of reflection. Think on the majesty and magnitude of God. Focus on the promises He has given you in His Word. Turn your attention to fulfilling His purpose for your life. Live in the confidence that He is in control. Relax, for there is nothing to worry about. God cares, and He keeps His promises to help.

Part 5

Promises for Your Triumph

14

Getting Your Prayers Answered

*G*etting results from prayer is one of our greatest concerns. Recently a man came to me and asked me to pray that he would get a certain position at work. "I really want that position," he announced abruptly. "I am praying that I will get it."

We prayed together and several weeks passed before I saw him again. "Did you get the job?" I asked.

"I prayed hard for that job," he replied, "but *just like I expected,* somebody else got it instead."

I thought to myself, *You got what you prayed for because what you expected is what you got!*

Too many of us treat prayer as if it were a routine spin of chance. *If I am lucky,* we think, *maybe God will say yes this time.* Unfortunately, that kind of halfhearted praying is going on all the time.

The Bible promises us that if we pray properly, we can be confident that God will answer us according to His will for us. Prayer is the most powerful force in our lives. It expresses the need of the human soul and touches the very heart of God Himself. Prayer is the most dynamic force available to us, and yet few of us truly pray. Those who have not learned to pray are living on a level below what God intended for them. Also, they are missing the greatest spiritual power they could ever know.

Only as we pray in faith will we begin to see God at work in our lives. Each of us must be willing to take God at His word and believe that He can do what He has promised to do for us. The God who can stop the sun or part the Red Sea can certainly answer our prayers.

I have found several key truths in Scripture that have made prayer work for me. I want to share them with you so they can work for you as well.

Understand God's Promises

The promises of God are clearly stated in Scripture. The key to obtaining them is faith. Jesus said, "All things are possible to him that believeth" (Mark 9:23). That is a promise of unlimited potential. Our ability to get our prayers answered is measured by our faith in God.

Faith is confidence in the integrity of God's promises. When we pray in faith, we are telling God that we trust His integrity. We are expressing that confidence by the very act of prayer itself. When we pray, we are communicating with the infinite and personal God who controls the entire universe. When you understand that, it takes the surprise out of answered prayer.

"Guess what, Pastor?" people will often say, "God answered my prayer!" They sound so surprised that God said yes. It shouldn't be that way; we ought to believe that He is going to answer our prayers and expect Him to do it!

Answered prayer is not so much a miracle as it is a fulfillment of God's spiritual laws. He has already promised that if we pray "according to His will" (1 John 5:14), He will grant our requests. This is a divine principle that always works. If my prayer is in submission to His will, I am going to get my prayer answered.

"What if I am asking for something that is not His will?" you may ask. Remember, if it isn't His will for your life, you don't want it. When I am willing to submit my desires to His plan and purpose alone, my life takes on even greater meaning and significance. By submitting, I am also placing the greatest possible faith in His integrity. That kind of praying says, "God, I trust You with my life even more than I trust myself."

*If your prayer is
in submission to His will,
you are going to get
your prayer answered.*

Faith is not the same as desire. Some people pray only for the things they desire, like a new house or a new car. Praying by faith is the kind of prayer that says, "God, let me know Your will about the car."

The *prayer of faith* trusts God to do what is best about the car. The *prayer of desire* says, "God, give me that car!" If we don't get it, we end up mad at God. That is not the prayer of faith, and God's refusal to answer it is not a failure on His part.

Prayer is also more than just positive thinking. I like positive thinkers, but positive thinking alone is no replacement for genuine prayer. I have often heard people say that they thought God was going to do something simply because *they* thought so. But that is not how God operates. We cannot force God to do things our way just because we think it is best for us.

When I was a little boy, we had another boy in our neighborhood who thought he was Superman. He had a very positive attitude about this belief. He even got his mother to buy him some blue leotards and make him a red cape and a yellow chest patch with a big, red "S" on it. He went around the neighborhood telling everyone that he was Superman. He was as positive and optimistic as he could be. In fact, he was so convincing that some of the children began to believe him.

"I'm Superman!" the boy said to everyone he met. But eventually, the day of reckoning came. One day another boy said, "If you are Superman, prove it!"

Caught in his own delusion, the boy insisted that he really was Superman.

"Then let's see you fly," replied his challenger. Tragically, little Superman climbed up on the neighbor's rooftop and jumped off in an attempt to fly. He hit the ground with a thud and broke his arm. All his positive thinking could not prevent his inevitable "collision" with the fact that he was not Superman.

Unfortunately, some of us treat God the same way. We think God is going to perform for us in a certain manner just because we think He ought to do it that way. We can beg, scheme, and manipulate, but if our request is not in accordance with God's will for our lives, He won't answer it. Real faith is simply believing that God will answer our prayers according to His will. It involves placing our trust in His integrity. Such prayer is the expression of our confidence in His character and our reliance upon His good intentions on our behalf.

Discover God's Direction

If the answer to our prayers must be in accord with God's will for our lives, then it is imperative that we clearly understand His will in any given situation. Fortunately, God does not leave the knowledge of His will up to guesswork. He has written a book explaining His will in great detail. That book is *the Bible.* Scripture clearly explains the will of God for the basic issues of life.

The discovery of God's will rests upon our clear understanding of the content and context of Scripture. The whole Word of God is the expression of His will and purpose for our lives. Therefore, every verse of Scripture must be interpreted in light of its context and in relation to the rest of Scripture. None of us have the right to take any passage out of context and attempt to interpret it for ourselves without viewing it in relation to the rest of revealed truth.

The apostle Paul wrote, "All scripture is given by inspiration of God, and is profitable for doctrine, for reproof, for correction, for instruction in righteousness: That the man of God may be perfect, throughly furnished unto all good works" (2 Timothy 3:16-17). Therefore, all 66 books of the Bible and each of the 1,189 chapters are inspired by God. Thus, the Bible is God's manual for successful living.

Before we ever begin praying, we need to refer to the instruction manual. Check the directions to see if you are moving in the right manner. Make sure your prayers are consistent with God's revealed truth. He won't answer a prayer that contradicts His own principles.

*God does not leave
the knowledge of His will
up to guesswork.*

We also need the guidance of *the Holy Spirit* in order to understand God's will for our lives. Jesus said, "Howbeit when he, the Spirit of truth, is come, he will guide you into all truth" (John 16:13). The Holy Spirit dwells in every believer's mind and heart. He uses the truth of Scripture to instruct, guide, convict, and encourage us in our daily walk with God. He leads us intuitively in the way we should go.

This does not mean that the Holy Spirit will lead us contrary to Scripture. Rather, He will guide us *to* the truth of Scripture that it might direct our lives in the way of the Lord. Remember, the will of God will always be consistent with the Word of God.

We also discover the will of God by developing *a sanctified mind*. As our minds are spiritually cleansed and renewed, they become proper receptacles for God's truth. You will never discover the will of God by reading secular magazines or watching secular television. Advice from the best secular minds falls far short of the revealed truth of the Word of God.

Finally, we can also find the will of God through *the doors of opportunity* which He opens to us. God is the one who opens and closes those doors for us. If a door of service is closed, then you can be sure that is not God's will for your life. If a door of service is open, that may well be His will for you. I say that with some reserve, realizing that God may open two or three doors of opportunity at the same time and you will have to choose one of them. Among those that are open to you, there may be more than one that is acceptable in His will, and you must choose between them. Most of the time, however, we don't have the privilege of more than one open door at a time, and it becomes evident that the one door of opportunity we have is indeed His will for us.

Sometimes it is not so important *who* you are as it is *where* you are in relation to finding God's will. It is more important that you be in the right place for Him to use you. I remember hearing a story several years ago about a state governor who went to visit a state mental hospital. While he was there, he needed to make a telephone call and asked to use a phone. He dialed the operator and said, "Hello, this is the governor. Please give me an outside line."

When the operator didn't answer, the governor began raising his voice and demanding an outside line.

Finally, in desperation, the governor asked, "Do you know who I am? This is the governor!"

The operator responded, "I don't know *who* you are, but I do know *where* you are!"

How long has it been since you put yourself in a proper place to hear from God? How long has it been since you searched the Scriptures and asked the Holy Spirit to reveal God's will for your life? How long has it been since you fasted and prayed and gave yourself totally over to God?

Only by this kind of determined searching can we discover God's perfect will for our lives. Don't give up the quest. Keep seeking; keep knocking; and keep searching. Remember, "this is the confidence that we have in him, that, if we ask any thing according to his will, he heareth us" (1 John 5:14).

Search for God's Illumination

There is nothing more frustrating than fumbling around in the dark. Sometimes it seems that is what we are doing as we search for the light of God's direction. A young business-man recently asked me, "Pastor, what can I do if I have read the Scripture, prayed fervently, and waited patiently for an answer to my prayers...but nothing has happened?"

I reminded him that there are times when we have done all we know to do and must be willing to pray in the light of truth that we have already. I may not know the totality of God's direction for my life, but I do know that I am moving ahead in the light I already have for now.

When the Babylonian king Nebuchadnezzar com-manded the Israelites to bow before his golden statue, three young Hebrews refused to do so. When Shadrach, Meshach, and Abednego stood their ground, they were threatened with being thrown into a fiery furnace. But in spite of their own fears, they replied, "If it be so, our God whom we serve is able to deliver us from the burning fiery furnace, and he will deliver us out of thine hand, O king. But if not, be it known unto thee, O king, that we will not serve thy gods, nor worship the golden image which thou hast set up" (Daniel 3:17-18).

Notice that these young men would not presume on the will of God. They were prepared to accept either option: life or death. Either would have been a form of deliverance from the wrath of the king. Both options were possible, and they were willing to accept either one in the will of God for their lives. They were trusting God's integrity and leaving the consequences in His hands.

During the war between the States, Confederate General Robert E. Lee went into a church and knelt to pray. When he left the church, someone asked him if he had prayed for the South to win the war. The general looked at him and said, "No, I wasn't praying for us to win. I was praying that God's will would be done." Now *that's* the way to pray!

*Prayer is the
heart of man calling out
to the heart of God.*

Prayer is not an easy process, even though there may be times when it seems easy to pray. There will also come difficult times when it is hard to pray. Such times will test your faith and stretch you to the limits of your humanity. But when you can pray even in the face of adversity, "Father...not my will, but thine, be done" (Luke 22:42), you can rest assured God will answer with that which is best for you.

Charles Spurgeon, the great Baptist pastor in the last century, said, "We may not always be able to trace the hand of God, but we can always trust the heart of God."

How can we be assured of getting our prayers answered? By learning to pray in faith. The key to answered prayer is a believing heart. The rest is up to God. Once we learn to pray understanding His promises and discovering His direction, the rest is a matter of trusting the light of revelation we have and walking by faith.

Prayer is a matter of the heart. It is the cry of a newborn child of God. It is the call for help when we are in trouble. It is the confident trust that we learn as mature believers. Praying is as natural to a Christian as breathing is to a baby. It is the heart of man calling out to the heart of God.

Pray in Jesus' Name

When I was a child, I often heard people end their prayers by saying, "In Jesus' name, Amen." I thought that was a nice, logical conclusion to their prayers. It seemed to me to work like "signing off" at the end of a broadcast. But I later learned that praying in Jesus' name is the most important element of our prayers. The name of Jesus is the very key to answered prayer.

You can pray without mentioning Jesus' name if you like, but you are missing out on the great power of prayer if you do. You can pray "for Jesus' sake" if you like, but prayer is not for His sake; it is for our sake. Praying in His name means that we are praying by His authority and in the power of His person. In fact, our Lord Himself taught us to pray in His name. He also promised great results if we would do just that.

In the ancient world, official requests were carried by hand and delivered in person. Those requests which were written as royal decrees carried the royal insignia. Those decrees which were delivered verbally were always given "in the name of" or "by the authority of" some prominent leader. This is the significance of praying in Jesus' name. Using His name acknowledges His lordship and authority in our lives.

What is the purpose of praying in Jesus' name? Our Lord Himself answered that question when He said, "Ask, and ye shall receive, that your joy may be full" (John 16:24). He wants to fill your life with the joy of His presence and power. He is delighted when we come to Him asking by faith in His name.

When a Christian has enough faith to bring his burdens and needs to the Savior, he is really saying, "Lord Jesus, I know that You love me and that You care about my problems." Our prayers in His name express our confidence in His character and our faith in His desire to meet our needs.

As we pray to God the Father, Jesus receives those prayers and expresses them to the Father. He might receive a prayer of mine and say, "Father, it's Richard again. He is praying for people to be saved today at Rehoboth Church."

"What gives him the authority to ask for this?" the Father might ask.

"He is asking it in My name," our Lord replies.

"Then let it be done," comes the Father's reply.

Never become weary in praying. Don't make the mistake of thinking you are bothering God with your requests. Every time you pray in Jesus' name, you are invoking the power of heaven on your behalf. Remember, the Bible says, "Ye have not, because ye ask not" (James 4:2). Start asking in Jesus' name, and see what happens. And remember, when you pray in His name, you are invoking His authority. Expect Him to answer!

15

A Reason for Hope

Several years ago a U.S. Navy submarine sank off the coast of Massachusetts in a terrible storm. With great haste, the Navy dispatched its finest rescue teams to the scene of the disaster. In time the divers located the ship and attempted to rescue the crew. For several hours their only means of contact with the crew trapped inside the submarine was by tapping on the hull with a metal instrument. The crew inside the submarine did the same, tapping out their messages by the dots and dashes of the Morse code.

Unfortunately, as the hours passed, the rescuers were unable to upright the vessel and set the crewmen free. Finally, the rescuers lost all contact with the crew inside the submerged submarine. The tapping signals stopped, and all was silent on the ocean floor. Then, in a faint and distant-sounding tap, the rescuers heard a crewman's desperate question: "Is there any hope? Is there any hope?"

As I watched the news account, my heart was filled with sorrow for these dying men. But I also thought of the **awful** spiritual plight of millions of people who are just as **desper**ately asking, "Is there any hope?"

I've heard it said that a person can live about 40 days without eating food, about four days without drinking water, and about eight minutes without breathing air—but a person can't live one minute without hope!

In a world of tension and confusion where it seems society has lost all sense of direction, we need to know that there is hope for our future. We need to know that there is something real and genuine to build our lives upon as we look ahead.

It is this kind of hope that Peter was reminding his readers of when he wrote about the "reason of the hope that is in you" (1 Peter 3:15). Peter realized that the confidence a Christian has in the face of life's difficulties is a hope the world does not understand. It is an inner spiritual confidence that goes beyond normal human comprehension.

The psalmist understood that same hope when he wrote Psalm 42. Though apparently he was discouraged and defeated at the time, he also realized God had not abandoned him without hope. As he struggled with life's toughest issues—the issues of the heart—he came to grips with life-changing truths. He found the reasons for hope. We can find them, too.

God's Presence Is with Us

As he searched his soul and uttered his prayer to God, the psalmist said, "My soul thirsteth for God" (Psalm 42:2). He realized that God was the living Lord. He understood that God, not he, was the ultimate reality. Our only significance lies not within ourselves, but in the fact that God lives with us.

Today, more than ever, people need to know that God is alive. They don't need more religion, statues, cornerstones, pillars, markers, churches, synagogues, or cathedrals. What they really need is a personal and spiritual encounter with the living God Himself!

As wonderful an institution as the church is in our society, I am afraid that many of us get so caught up in our denominational affiliations that we forget all about God. I am also concerned that we often get so entangled in the redundancy of the form and ritual of religion that we miss God altogether. He is just as alive and real as you, your best friend, or family member are.

Unfortunately, most of us don't think of God in such personal terms. We tend to view Him as an abstraction sort of floating around "out there." But God is not some vague theological or philosophical abstraction. He is real, alive, and personal. He is not just some obscure idea to be treated with irreverence and disrespect. But many people treat Him that way because they do not realize who He is.

Vance Havner, author and evangelist, tells the story of a young girl who once toured the great museums of Europe (*The Vance Havner Notebook,* Grand Rapids, MI: Baker Book House, p. 224). Eventually, she came to a museum in Venice that housed Beethoven's piano. Intrigued by this great piano, she sat down at it and began to play some rock and roll. A caretaker heard her banging on the keys and rushed over and said, "Miss, do you know whose piano this is?"

"Yes, it's Beethoven's piano," she said.

"Then why are you playing it?" the caretaker asked.

"Oh, I like playing the piano," she said.

"Let me tell you something," he responded. "The other day, Paderewski, the great pianist, came here to see Beethoven's piano."

"What did he play?" asked the girl.

"Nothing," the caretaker explained. "Paderewski said he was not worthy to touch Beethoven's piano."

Too many of us are like this foolish girl when it comes to dealing with God. We impersonalize Him, and then we irreverently trivialize Him. We tend to become flippant about the things of God when we forget how real He is. He is not "out there" somewhere. Yes, He is the ruler of the universe. But He is also the personal and infinite God who cares about each one of us.

The greatest hope for mankind is the knowledge of God as a real, personal, and living Savior. His very presence in our lives reminds us that we are not alone as we face the future. God is on our side.

God's Face Is Toward Us

As the psalmist struggled in prayer in Psalm 42, he asked the searching question, "Why art thou cast down, O my soul? And why art thou disquieted in me? Hope thou in God: for I shall yet praise him for the help of his countenance" (verse 5). I have often taken great hope in this passage myself. Notice the beautiful sentiment that it expresses: We can hope in God because His face is toward us. He is interested in our lives, our needs, and our problems. He is looking, gazing, and watching intently to make sure that our every need is met.

"Countenance" is another word for face. As we study the Psalms, we see that term used again and again. In Psalm 27:8, David said, "Thy face, LORD, will I seek." In Psalm 31:16, he prayed, "Make thy face to shine upon thy servant." David was saying, "God, look at me, and I know everything will be well."

In my book *The Unfailing Promise* (Word Books, 1988), I told the story of a young preacher, 37 years old, whose beautiful wife died from an incurable disease. As the young pastor and his little daughter left her graveside grieving and sobbing, they clung to each other all the way home. Later that evening, the little girl asked if she could sleep with her father because she was afraid without her mother.

So they crawled into bed, pulled up the covers, and turned off the light. Soon the young pastor, exhausted by the pressure of all he had endured, was fast asleep. But after a few minutes, he was awakened when he felt the tiny fingers of his little daughter on his face.

"What's wrong, honey?" he asked.

"Nothing," she replied. "Daddy, I'm just feeling to see if your face is toward me."

You and I as believers can rest assured that God's face is always toward us. He loves us with a personal love that will not let us go. In our darkest and most difficult moment, He is there to assure us of His love. The God who sent His Son to die for your sins loves you enough to keep you through your toughest times.

God's Strength Is Within Us

Every born-again child of God realizes that the Spirit of God dwells within him or her. Once He has entered our lives by faith, He takes up residence within us. God lives within the human soul of redeemed men and women.

Realizing who and what we are in God will revolutionize the way we live.

Thus, the psalmist prayed, "O my God, my soul is cast down within me: therefore will I remember thee" (Psalm 42:6). Despite his own discouragement, he turned his attention to God. He remembered who God was and what a difference He could make in his life. He had to remind himself of who God was and, therefore, who he was as a child of God.

Realizing *who* and *what* we are in God will revolutionize the way we live. When times of discouragement engulf us, we must understand that the living God is within us to empower us to do His will. We are not just imitators of God, trying to do the best we can for Him. We are the living, breathing, walking, and talking children of the Almighty God.

God spoke to the prophet Ezekiel concerning His people, saying, "I will give them one heart, and I will put a new spirit within you; and I will take the stony heart out of their flesh, and will give them an heart of flesh: That they may walk in my statutes, and keep mine ordinances, and do them: and they shall be my people, and I will be their God" (Ezekiel 11:19-20).

What is this new Spirit that will cause our hearts to be changed? It is the empowering Holy Spirit of Almighty God! Before our Lord Jesus went into heaven, He told us of the Holy Spirit who would come. He said, "The Comforter, which is the Holy Ghost, whom the Father will send in my name, he shall teach you all things" (John 14:26). And it is the sweet and powerful presence of His Holy Spirit that makes God's power available to us. What a promise, and what a hope! He is the source of our love, our joy, and our peace. He is the one who enables us to overcome all the trials and temptations of life. When we realize that we are not alone because God's presence is not only *with* us but He is also *within* us, we ought to be the most powerful and positive people on earth.

We should be like the little boy who kept tossing a baseball into the air and trying to hit it with his bat. He tried time and time again and missed the ball every time.

"Son, you're not much of a hitter," called out an old man watching his attempts.

"No, sir," said the little boy, "but, wow, am I ever a pitcher!"

No matter what pressures, problems, or struggles we may face in life, Christians have every reason to be positive because our lives are indwelt by the Holy Spirit, empowered of God, and destined for heaven. He is both *with* us and *in* us. He is *watching over* us and *working in* us at the same time. The living God has poured His Spirit and presence within us; therefore, we have every reason to hope. It is no wonder the Bible calls us "more than conquerers" in Christ (Romans 8:37).

God's Lovingkindness Watches Over Us

In Psalm 42:8, we read, "Yet the LORD will command his lovingkindness in the daytime, and in the night his song shall be with me." There is never a time, day or night, when we are not in His loving care. He always watches over us with His lovingkindness. He is always with us, and we are never left alone to struggle for ourselves without His help.

*The same God who is with us
on the mountaintops of life
is with us in the valleys.*

Recently I was a guest on several radio and television programs in Los Angeles. One of the stations, I was told, is the most listened-to Christian station in America. We were doing a call-in response program where listeners could call the station to ask me a question on the air. One dear lady called in and asked, "Dr. Lee, is it wrong for me to call upon God in my hour of need?"

This lady was so discouraged and dejected that she was even questioning whether she should call upon God for help at all. "Is He really there? Can He help me?" she asked desperately.

"Certainly," I said. "Not only is He really there, but it blesses the heart of God to answer His children in their hour of need!"

The same God, who is with us on the mountaintops of life, is also there walking beside us through the valleys. He is always the same, whether we are up or down. He is the Friend who sticks closer to us than a brother. He has promised, "I will never leave thee, nor forsake thee" (Hebrews 13:5). He also said, "Call unto me, and I will answer thee, and shew thee great and mighty things" (Jeremiah 33:3).

The invitations in Scripture are many. Time and again we hear God calling us to come to Him and lean on Him because He cares for us. In 2 Chronicles 16:9 we read, "The eyes of the LORD run to and fro throughout the whole earth, to shew himself strong in the behalf of them whose heart is perfect toward him." Notice again that God's face is toward us and His gaze is intent. He is looking for someone to bless, to love, and to give hope in his or her moment of despair.

Charles Wesley, one of the founding fathers of the Methodist Church and the brother of the famous evangelist John Wesley, was walking beside a lake one day when a terrible storm arose. The wind grew fierce, the sky dark, the lightning flashed, and thunder roared as the terrible storm approached. Suddenly, a frightened little bird, tossed about by the wind, flew under Wesley's coat. There it remained, shivering in fear, until the storm was over. Finally, Wesley reached in, removed the little bird from its place of shelter, and released it into the calm blue sky. As he thought about the bird and its place of safety, he took his pen and wrote these familiar words:

> Jesus, Lover of my soul,
> Let me to Thy bosom fly.
> While the nearer waters roll,
> While the tempest still is high!
> Hide me, O my Savior, hide,
> Till the storm of life is past;
> Safe into thy haven guide,
> O receive my soul at last!

God's Hope Is for Us

The psalmist ends by proclaiming God to be "my rock" (Psalm 42:9), and then announces a final challenge: "Hope thou in God: for I shall yet praise him" (verse 11). He saw that God was his only hope and sure foundation—a certain hope that would never fail.

There is a famous painting by G.F. Watt that is entitled "Hope." In it is the scene of a woman who has had to battle life. She is pictured as beaten and worn. She is holding a harp on which all the strings are broken but one. That one string is called the string of hope. She is shown striking that one string, and as she does, the music of hope fills her world. In the midst of her struggle she has found the string of hope, and that has made her life worth living.

For every man the music of hope is found in Jesus Christ. If someone were to ask you, "Where is your hope today?" what would you reply? Is your hope in your religion, your good deeds, your career, your health, your money? Or is your hope in the living God and the power found in His eternal salvation? The greatest issue of the heart and life is the answer to that question. God is waiting for those who will call upon Him to be with them, to turn His face toward them, to dwell within them, and to keep them safe in His everlasting care. Now that is a hope worth living for, and a hope that is available for all who are willing to receive it through faith in Jesus Christ.

If your heart is hurting, there's hope in Jesus Christ. He is the Healer of broken hearts. If your life is shattered and crushed, turn it over to Him. He will take those broken pieces and mold them together into a brand-new life.

Hope is never lost where there is a Savior who is still waiting to meet your needs.

Other Good
Harvest House Reading

EMBRACING GOD
by *David Swartz*

"Every good and perfect gift is from above, coming down from the Father," the apostle James exclaimed. Surprisingly, many Christians are innocently unaware of the many shapes these gifts take. We expect one thing, while all the time God has so much more in store for us! *Embracing God* is a compassionate invitation to intimacy with the Father.

LIFETIME GUARANTEE
by *Bill Gillham*

You've tried fixing your marriage, your kids, your job. Suddenly the light dawns. It's not your *problems* that need to be fixed—it's your *life*! The good news is that God doesn't ask you to live *your* life for Christ, but to let Him live *His* life through you. With humor, candor, and "plain vanilla talk," author Bill Gillham takes a new and enlightening look at the concept of your identity *in Christ*.

WHEN LIFE ISN'T FAIR
by *Dwight Carlson* and *Susan Carlson Wood*

Blending personal experience and theological insight, along with Dr. Carlson's extensive background in medicine and psychology, the authors present a deeply moving study of the whys and causes of physical and emotional suffering.

LOVING GOD WITH ALL YOUR MIND
by *Elizabeth George*

"Biblical thinking," writes author Elizabeth George, "gives women freedom from the draining emotions of fear, worry, depression, and bitterness." Liz will help you develop a scriptural and healthy view of God, the past, the future, problems, other people, and yourself, based on six truths backed by God's promises and power.